Brave New Discipleship

CULTIVATING SCRIPTURE-DRIVEN
CHRISTIANS IN A CULTURE-DRIVEN WORLD

MAX ANDERS

THOMAS NELSON
Since 1798

NASHVILLE   MEXICO CITY   RIO DE JANEIRO

Published in Nashville, Tennessee, by Thomas Nelson. Thomas Nelson is a registered trademark of HarperCollins Christian Publishing.

Author represented by Erik S. Woglemuth; Woglemuth and Associates, Inc.

Page design and layout: Crosslin Creative

Thomas Nelson titles may be purchased in bulk for educational, business, fund-raising, or sales promotional use. For information, please e-mail SpecialMarkets@ThomasNelson.com.

Unless otherwise noted, Scripture quotations are taken from the NEW AMERICAN STANDARD BIBLE®, Copyright © The Lockman Foundation 1960, 1962, 1963, 1968, 1971, 1972, 1973, 1975, 1977, 1995. Used by permission.

ISBN: 978-0-7180-3064-3

Printed in the United States of America

15 16 17 18 19 20 [RRD] 6 5 4 3 2 1

This book is dedicated to Dr. Howard Hendricks
and Dr. E. William Male, two men who believed in me, and
without whom this book could not have been written.

Contents

3. implement with disciplers of the highest spiritual standards.

That is the challenge of discipleship in the twenty-first century. And that is the intent of this book, to explore and define more effective ways of discipling in a radically different world.

To begin, I want to define terms. There is no technical definition of discipleship, and so I want to define how I am using the term, so as not to miscommunicate. I define *discipleship* as giving a willing person the assistance necessary to grow to maturity in Christ. I take this comprehensive idea from Matthew 28:19–20. Because of the comprehensive nature of this definition, the common idea of discipleship—that of one person pouring his life into the lives of a few other individuals—is not adequate. In my opinion, there is no one person who is capable of giving another person all the assistance that person will need to become mature in Christ. Therefore, discipleship is the work of the church as a whole, as I see it.

However, it is essential that individuals pour their lives into the lives of a few others. That is a vital part of discipleship. But it does not equal the whole of discipleship. Therefore, I define that activity as *mentoring*. That way, I do not have to use one word—discipleship—to refer to both things.

Therefore, here are my definitions. They are not right and other definitions wrong, but they keep us on the same page.

Discipleship: giving a willing person the assistance needed to grow to maturity in Christ. (The work of the church as a whole.)

Mentoring: a more experienced Christian, through personal relationship, encouraging and coaching a less experienced Christian in growing spiritually. (The work of called and qualified individuals.)

I will also be making some evaluative statements about the value of modern electronic media. Of course, the actual electronic media . . . computers, internet, smart phones, etc. . . . are neither bad nor good. They are merely information devices. What makes them harmful or helpful is the information transmitted through them. I will make the case that actual electronic media can, and must, be used for good if we are to meet the demands of 21st Century discipleship.

With that foundation of understanding having been laid, let us begin.

CHAPTER 1

Central Passage: "All these men [from the tribe of Issachar] understood the signs of the times . . ." (1 Chron. 12:32 NLT).

Discipleship in the Twenty-First Century Presents Unprecedented Challenges

The pervasiveness of electronic communication presents a multipronged challenge to the cultivation of a vital inner life, creating new demands for discipleship.

I am deeply concerned that the church seems to be losing ground in producing mature followers of Christ. I do not see our discipleship process in the early part of the twenty-first century as being very effective. It is not that there is anything inherently wrong with traditional discipleship methodology, but that time has moved on, and I am not sure the church has moved adequately with it when it comes to discipleship.

I fear that the typical education and discipleship approach used in the United States today is doomed because it does not match up with the characteristics of newer generations. It is not that typical material and approaches are useless. Fortunately, there will always be those who are willing and able to adapt themselves to the more traditional methods and materials. But when it comes to reaching a broad spectrum and large number of typical Christians today, I fear that the methods and materials of the past will prove ineffective for the future.

Perhaps the greatest challenge facing the church in America today is the shallowization of the church. For the last couple of decades many of us have read the statistics produced by the Barna Group and other polling groups that show the attitudes, values, and behavior of Christians not being statistically significantly different from non-Christians. Christians are supposed to be different from the world, but as a category, we are not—or at best there may be a five- or ten-year lag. Research indicates that not only are we losing our distinctive lifestyle, but we are also beginning to lose our distinctive beliefs on which a distinctive lifestyle is built. Pastors of some of the nation's largest churches describe their congregations as "a mile wide and an inch deep."

This would be a significant problem even if the historically Christian culture in the United States were remaining constant. But that is not the case. It is collapsing like a burned-out barn, which means that Christians are collapsing with it, making it spiritually catastrophic.

Christian author Dallas Willard has written that Christians are shallow, not in spite of what the church is doing, but precisely because of what the church is doing. He applied the well-known business maxim to the church: "the system you have in place is perfectly designed to produce the results you are getting."[1] If we want different results, he contends we must use a different system.

> Perhaps the greatest challenge facing the church in America today is the shallowization of the church.

interpret the present as normal. Because of this, the church is in danger of being neutralized by a mind-meld with modern culture. As a result, we must create a new approach to discipleship if we are going to be able to help younger generations of Christians withstand the gravitational pull of modern culture.

This new discipleship strategy must address all areas of the Christian life. It used to be that discipleship could hit the high points of the Christian life, like a spiritual finishing school, and count on Christianized American culture to fill in the gaps. For example, fifty years ago, if you conformed to American pop culture, you did not live in violation of any of the Ten Commandments. Today, however, if you conform to American pop culture, you may frequently violate most of the Ten Commandments. As a result, not only can we not assume that Christianized American culture will fill in the gaps of anything we do not cover in our discipleship system with values that are congruent with Christianity, but rather we must assume that secularized American culture will fill in the gaps with values that are hostile to Christianity. Therefore, the church must be intentional about every single thing it wants to see happen in the life of a disciple. Nothing significant can be left to chance.

We cannot just teach the Bible. We cannot just mentor for Christlike lifestyle. We cannot just train for Christian ministry. We must do all three, and we must do them in the most effective way, with the most effective methodology. There are effective ways to teach the Bible and ineffective ways. There are effective ways to influence character, and there are ineffective ways. There are effective ways to equip people for ministry, and there are ineffective ways. We do not have the luxury of remaining entrenched in ineffective ways.

The church must:

1. match comprehensive ministry goals with

2. the most effective ministry methods and

Introduction

The Brave New World of the twenty-first century requires a Brave New Discipleship strategy to meet the new demands.

Twentieth-century discipleship models will not effectively translate into twenty-first-century culture. The purpose of this book is to rethink, reimagine, and articulate a discipleship strategy equal to the demands of the new spiritual territory in which we find ourselves in the twenty-first century.

In 1948, George Orwell wrote a dystopian novel entitled *1984*. In it he imagined a very unpleasant future in which everything we wanted was kept from us by a totalitarian government.

In contrast, in 1931, Aldous Huxley wrote a dystopian novel entitled *Brave New World* in which he imagined a very unpleasant future resulting not from things being withheld from us, but from everything being made available to us, regardless of its value. With the glut of things available, regardless of their value, culture and society began to sink to the level of the lowest appetites.

Of the two contrasting visions of the future, Huxley's is the one coming true for us in the West. A quick glance at the programs on cable television is, perhaps, the most obvious indication of this. From boundless violence to unrestrained and perverted sex, to voyeuristic explorations into unrefined and deviant lifestyles, cable television is showing us the future. It is not a pretty sight.

It is my belief that twentieth-century models of discipleship will not effectively translate widely into this Brave New World of twenty-first-century culture. Older generations look on in horror at our speed-of-light cultural deterioration, like watching a train wreck happen. But younger generations are less horrified, more ready to

How to Get the Most from This Book

1. Whether or not you are discipling others, you can also use the principles in this book to disciple yourself. As you read about principles of discipling others, it will be easy for you to make the connection of how you would guide and accelerate your own spiritual growth by applying the principles to your own spiritual maturation process. This idea is explored more fully in the last chapter of the book, after you have had a chance to become familiar with the principles.

2. There are exercises at the end of each chapter that are designed to increase your memory, understanding, and application of the material in the chapter.

3. The exercises seem simple, and they are. But they are also important. They will deepen the learning experience significantly if they are done with care. Please avail yourself of the opportunity.

4. There are boldface words and sentences in the text. They correspond to the exercises at the end of the chapter. Notice them as you read, and it will be easier to complete the exercises.

5. If you are teaching this book, you can also use these exercises for sharing times, discussion, and assignments. This, too, will significantly increase the educational impact of the book.

Believe me, this is not a criticism. I have struggled for decades to analyze and decipher what is happening to the church and what to do about it. But in this context, it is time to ask ourselves, *In our age of rapid and massive change, is our discipleship system producing disciples who know the Bible well—who have mastered the Bible so well that the Bible masters them?*

Is our discipleship system producing disciples whose character reflects Christ—who are holy toward God and loving toward others, whose lives are separated from sin, dedicated to biblical pursuits, and committed to eternal reality?

Is our discipleship system producing disciples who have dedicated their resources of time, talent, and treasure to the service of others, helping extend the kingdom of light into the kingdom of darkness around us?

There are many extraordinary examples of people who do just that. But evidence suggests that on the whole, the church is dramatically falling short on discipleship. As I speak with people about this subject, there seems to be a pervasive sense among church observers that we are categorically failing at this central responsibility.

The reasons are complex. But one reason is that **it may be generally more difficult to live the Christian life in the twenty-first century than at any other time in history. This is, in part, because of the pervasiveness and power of electronic communication.** From music in elevators to television monitors and touch screens in taxis to smart phones, tablets, computers, electronic games, smart watches, and televisions that often go on first thing in the morning and stay on until the last thing at night, our minds are awash in input from electronic media. And because we become what we behold, we are dramatically impacted by the pervasive presence of electronic media.

This creates two serious problems. First, it gives the mind no downtime, no solitude, no time for reflection, planning, evaluating, or thinking. The result is that it is very difficult to conceive of higher things, to rise above where we are at the moment. We get trapped in the present with little hope for the future because we give no thought to it.

Second, the input that we receive is often godless. By *godless*, two things are meant. On the one hand, it may be an affront to the moral standards of God. The input may include violence, hatred, greed, and sexual immorality. On the other hand, even if the input is not an obvious affront to God, media typically represents life and values that do not include God or accurately reflect Him. So, even if a given program on television is not morally reprehensible, it still tends to teach us to think and live without God because an accurate and authentic relationship with God is virtually never modeled. All we ever learn by example is how to live without Him.

In addition, electronic media impacts the mind more than other forms of spoken or written communication. Have you ever tried to read a book while the television is on? You usually wind up watching television. Electronic media takes over the mind. That is why it is so powerful.

Therefore, because (1) electronic media keeps us from thinking about the higher things of life, (2) much of its input is godless, and (3) it has a greater power over the mind than other forms of spoken or written communication, the typical mind in Western culture is held captive by electronic media. As a result, the mind is held captive to secular values and thinking. Unfortunately, this is true of the Christian mind as well as the non-Christian mind.

In a dramatic instance of the impact of electronic media, I was presenting workshops at a discipleship conference in England a number of years ago. Delegates were there from all over the world. In one of my workshops, there was a delegation from central Africa, and after the session was over, we sat around talking about discipleship issues. This delegation said that their mission was to try to reach the rural villages in central Africa with the gospel before the village got electricity because before a village got electricity, their interest in spiritual things was very high. After a village got electricity, however, their interest in spiritual things dried up almost overnight because electricity brought not only lightbulbs and refrigeration but also television, movies, music, and the Internet. These things captured the minds of the villagers and made them almost impervious to the gospel. Like trying to save people from a coming tsunami, this delegation was trying to save rural central Africans from the coming tsunami of electrification.

Such is the power of electronic media in the twenty-first century.

While this instance provides a compelling example of the power of electronic media, its influence on our nation has been less obvious than electrification in central Africa but just as impacting, and it is a reality to which we must respond.

The goal of discipleship—giving someone the assistance needed to be conformed into the character image of Christ—will never change, but the methodology will and must. This Brave New World into which we are entering requires a Brave New Discipleship strategy if the church is not to be neutralized by a mind-meld with modern culture from overexposure to electronic media. Christians must either pull away from modern culture and isolate themselves from electronic media (which is not likely to happen), or they must find ways of offsetting the pervasiveness and power of electronic media as well as ways to use the same technology that is drawing people away from Christ to draw them to Christ. This is a massive and difficult challenge, not easily met. But it can and must be done.

> The goal of discipleship . . . will never change, but the methodology will and must.

Review for Memory (consult pages 3–5 for verification)

1. It may be generally more d_*ifficult*_____ to live the Christian life in the twenty-first century than at any other time in history. (Page 3)

2. One reason is the p_*ervasiveness*_____ and p_*ower*_____ of electronic communication. (Page 3)

3. This creates two serious problems. First, it gives the mind no d_*owntime*_____, no solitude, no time for reflection, planning, evaluating, or thinking. Second, the input we get is often g_*odless*_____. (Pages 3–4)

4. The g_*oal*_____ of discipleship will never change . . . giving people the assistance needed to be conformed into the character image of Christ . . . but the m_*ethodology*_____ will and must. (Page 5)

Review for Understanding

In your own words, state the challenge that the church faces concerning discipleship today.

We can't escape the ungodly influence of media + electronics, and it is subtly but powerfully blurring the lines between Christian distinctive values/behaviors + the world's.

Review for Application

Reflecting on the experience of the delegation from central Africa (pages 4–5), what have you personally observed or experienced regarding the harmful effects of electronic media in the Christian life?

- Lack of true presence in "quality time" w/ others.
- Inability to be still, to enjoy silence/solitude.
- Comparison + parading a mask rather than being real about sin + struggle... shift to focus on appearance vs. image of Christ in each other.

CHAPTER 2

Central Passage: *"Whatever is true, whatever is honorable, whatever is right, whatever is pure, whatever is lovely, whatever is of good repute, if there is any excellence and if anything worthy of praise, dwell on these things" (Phil. 4:8).*

We Become What We Behold

We automatically become like what we put into our minds and what we allow our minds to dwell on. Therefore, we must strategically guard our minds.

When it comes to being a fully devoted follower of Christ, would you like to be more than you are? Boy, I would. I long to be more than I am. I would like to know more. I long to be stronger spiritually. I long to be kinder, more patient, less influenced by negative emotions, more helpful to other people, more self-disciplined, more trusting and readily-obedient to all God asks of me, and to have greater vision and effectiveness in ministry. We should never stop wanting to be more like Christ.

This is important because we will never help others become fully devoted followers of Christ unless we are fully devoted followers of Christ ourselves, and we will never be fully devoted followers of Christ ourselves until we have mastered the challenge of personal growth in the spiritually toxic twenty-first century.

We set the high-water mark for our ministries. There are a few people who may go beyond us spiritually, almost no matter how poorly we disciple. And there are a few who will go nowhere spiritually, almost no matter how well we disciple. But the vast majority in between is the benchmark for our ministry. For the most part, they will be influenced by us but will not go beyond us. Therefore, if we want others to rain, we must have a cloudburst. If we want them to burn, we must combust. So, when it comes to pondering the effectiveness of discipleship in the twenty-first century, the first place we must look is in the mirror.

The Challenge of Modern Culture

Being the model we should be is not a simple task, however. Becoming spiritually mature has never been a quick or easy process. And it is made even more difficult in our age by the culture we live in. Our culture, which for hundreds of years was dominated by biblical values, has in the last fifty years been severely compromised by secular values. The magnitude and speed of the compromise has been fueled by the pervasiveness and toxic quality of much electronic communication, especially in recent years.

Peggy Noonan, former speechwriter for President Reagan and now a best-selling author, news analyst, and commentator, writes in her book *Life, Liberty and the Pursuit of Happiness*:

> We are the inheritors of a coarsened society. My generation cooperated happily in the coarsening, of course, in the sixties and seventies . . . and now we're stuck with it. The coarsened nation is what we're left with to bring up our children. A coarse place is by definition anti-child because it is anti-innocence.[1]

Parents today go to great lengths to protect their children from the environment that they helped create. However, there are not enough good parents to go around any more, not enough good parents to take up the slack. There is only the "coarsened society" that is making things worse.

The old culture may have been a little naïve, but in those early days of television, there were game shows, Saturday morning cartoons, nature shows on PBS, old movies, art and language lessons, and soap operas. Not very imaginative or sophisticated, but as Noonan points out, "That is better than today when the Geto Boys on channel 25 rap about killing women, having sex with their dead bodies, and cutting off their breasts."[2]

Ms. Noonan goes on to write,

> Really, you have to . . . know that this stuff is harmful, that it damages the young, the unsteady, the unfinished. You have to not care about anyone to sing these words and put this song on TV for money. You have to be a pig. . . .
>
> Hollywood knows it encourages and discourages points of view, habits, and social tendencies. And deep in their guilty little hearts, filmmakers know they encourage violence in men and boys and sexual acting out in everyone else. It's what they do for a living.[3]

After shocking and violating everyone on one level so that they get used to it, Hollywood has to come up with even more violence, perversion, and sex to hold a jaded audience's attention. How destructive that is to the individual soul! How destructive it is to the collective soul of our nation!

So, this is the world in which we now live. It has been deeply corrupted from what it once was, and the corruption is largely initiated in the entertainment industry and disseminated primarily through electronic media. And this coarsened culture has its automatic effect on us, whether we want it to or not. No one falls in a vat of ink without turning a little blue.

The Promise of Scripture

Even though modern culture makes committed Christian behavior a significant challenge, God has not left us without offsetting spiritual resources. Scripture says, "No temptation has overtaken you but such as is common to man; and God is faithful, who will not allow you to be tempted beyond what you are able, but with the temptation will provide the way of escape also, so that you will be able to endure it" (1 Cor. 10:13).

God has not allowed us to blunder into a situation that Christ is not sufficient for. He has not left us to fend for ourselves. God has, in order to offset this historic challenge, provided historic counterbalancing resources so that if a Christian walks wisely in this world, it is still possible to live an authentic Christian life of peace and power. But if we do not avail ourselves of resources God has made available to us, we can be swept like a cork down the stream of life.

Because electronic media is such a powerful influence on the Christian life, we cannot deal with being balanced in an unbalanced world without addressing it.

The Power of Choice

1. We Become What We Behold: Every moment of every day, something in our soul is being fed and something is being starved. As a result, we inevitably become what we think about and what we let into our minds. This fact caused nineteenth-century English poet William Blake to write, "We become what we behold." This phrase was picked up and popularized by culture-guru Marshall McLuhan in the 1960s and is verified powerfully by the modern study of the brain.

Impressions travel along pathways in the brain to various destinations in the brain. The more often an impression travels the pathway, the deeper that pathway becomes. The deeper that pathway becomes, the more it controls our attitudes, values, and behavior. For that reason, when something is reinforced in our mind over and over again, it affects how we think, feel, and behave. When the attitudes, values, and behavior of modern culture wash through our minds over and over again, they wear deep pathways in our brains,

[handwritten margin note: Wow. This really puts it into stark reality.]

[handwritten margin note: This is fascinating!]

powerfully influencing our own attitudes, values and behaviors on a subconscious level. That is, we might say, drawing on our conscious mind, that we have one set of beliefs based on the Bible and yet live by a completely different set of values based in our subconscious mind.

So, in our conscious mind, we may be fully aware of the passage of scripture that says, "My God will supply all your needs according to His riches in glory in Christ Jesus" (Phil. 4:19), a passage that should give us comfort and peace in the face of financial difficulties. Yet, when we face financial ruin, we are often wracked with fear, anxiety, worry, and distress because of the values lodged in our subconscious mind, which governs our attitudes, values, and behavior.

> . . . if [Paul] focused on the things that are seen, he would lose heart.

So, in understanding that the more often thoughts travel along pathways in the brain the more they affect our true attitudes, values, and behavior, we need to use that fact to work for us rather than against us.

In 2 Corinthians 4:16–18, the apostle Paul wrote:

> Therefore we do not lose heart, but though our outer man is decaying, yet our inner man is being renewed day by day. For momentary, light affliction is producing for us an eternal weight of glory far beyond all comparison, while we look not at the things which are seen, but at the things which are not seen; for the things which are seen are temporal, but the things which are not seen are eternal.

In this passage, we see that Paul did not lose heart because he focused "not [on] the things which are seen, but [on] the things which are not seen" (1 Cor. 4:18). The opposite would also be true—if he focused on the things that are seen, he would lose heart. So, what we behold—in this case, what we think about over and over again—can determine whether we lose heart or not in the face of affliction.

Breakthroughs in the last ten years in our understanding of how the brain works make it clear that when we think something over and over again, that thought becomes more and more deeply ingrained in our brain. If we mentally rehearse thoughts over and over again, day after day, week after week, month after month, those thoughts become deeply ingrained in our mind and begin to have a profound impact on our beliefs.

This works for us if we are reinforcing helpful beliefs. It works against us if we are reinforcing unhelpful beliefs. The problem is that in living in the world around us, negative beliefs are automatically reinforced. It cannot be avoided. I remember hearing Billy Graham once say that his grandchildren faced more temptation going to school on Monday morning than he and his friends could find driving around looking for it on Friday nights when he was a young boy.

Mary Pipher has written in her book *The Shelter of Each Other*, regarding media:

> Families are old institutions with very new problems. For the first time in two thousand years of Western civilization, families live in houses without walls. That is, they live in a world in which walls no longer offer protection. Technology has brought the outside world into the living room. Electronic media seeps into the [openings] of homes and teaches children ways of thinking, feeling, and behaving that are at odds with common sense. Families are reeling under the pressure of a culture they can't control. . . . We must remember that all television is educational. It teaches values and behavior. Children learn these things from ads; that they are the most important person in the universe, that impulses are not to be denied, that pain should not be tolerated, that the cure for any kind of pain is a product. They learn a weird mix of dissatisfaction and entitlement. With the messages of ads, we are socializing children to be self-centered, impulsive, and addictive. The television that Leonard Cohen called "that hopeless little screen" teaches values as clearly as any church.[4]

Neil Postman has written a compelling book regarding the impact of television on modern life titled *Amusing Ourselves to Death*.[5] The most powerful conclusion we can come to from reading it is that the first step in breaking the hold of television is realizing that it has a hold on us. That is one of the major points I want to make regarding the full range of modern media today: it has a hold on us, the hold is largely bad, and the first step in breaking that hold is recognizing that it has a hold.

So, we become what we behold, and unless we move to a remote, fenced-in compound without electricity in northern Montana, we are beholding plenty of harmful input from electronic media in the living of our everyday life, and are being negatively affected by it.

2. Therefore, Choose What You Want to Become: The tendency for people who start out with this kind of message is to get wild-eyed and shout, "Smash the televisions, burn the DVDs, blow up the computers!" That option is not all bad, but it is not realistic. First, many people would not be able to keep their jobs or function with effectiveness if they eliminated electronic media from their lives. Second, most people do not have the willpower to do so. Plus, there is a world of good available through electronic media that would be lost. (I could not possibly have the ministry I have today without electronic media.) The better alternative is to learn to control media so that it can work for you and not against you.

Two questions that helped break the hold of media addiction in my life are:

1. What do you want out of life?

2. Are you willing to pay the price?

Those two questions have to go together because if we only ask what we want out of life, it is just daydreaming unless we are willing to pay the price. But if we are willing to pay the price, then a world of possibilities opens up to us. If we decide ahead of time that we want an authentic Christian life marked by love, joy, peace, and power, if that is what we decide we want, and if we decide that we are willing to pay the price, then many of the decisions we face in life will have already been made, even before we face them.

The Bible talks a great deal about commitment and dedication:

I discipline my body and make it my slave, so that, after I have preached to others, I myself will not be disqualified. (1 Cor. 9:27)

I have been crucified with Christ; and it is no longer I who live, but Christ lives in me; and the *life* which I now live in the flesh I live by faith in the Son God who loved me and gave Himself up for me. (Gal. 2:20)

Therefore I urge you, brethren, by the mercies of God, to present your bodies a living and holy sacrifice, acceptable to God, *which is* your spiritual service of worship. (Rom. 12:1)

Half-hearted measures yield half-hearted results. Only whole-hearted measures will yield whole-hearted results. So, when we choose what we want to become, and make a life commitment to it, there is great power released in our lives. Within reason, we can have what we want. But we must choose it. We must decide what we want out of life and be willing to pay the price.

I would like to use my own experience as an example. I have lived long enough to have compiled a history of how things go when I live biblically and how things go when I do not live biblically. When I live biblically, I get the fruit that the Bible promises: love, joy, and peace. When I live unbiblically, I get the opposite: animosity, frustration, and conflict.

It was out of that firsthand experience that I learned that everything God asks of us, He does so to give something good to us and keep some harm from us. Therefore, the shortest distance between us and the life we long for is total obedience to Christ.

Many Christians do not believe that. I know I did not believe it for years. I would have gotten it right on a true/false test, but I proved that I did not believe it by how I lived, trying to combine a little of God and a little of my own plans, work, and effort. But that approach got me kicked around pretty hard by life and kicked around so long that I finally decided to give faith and obedience a try.

Over time, the Lord has honored the commitment and led me to a place that is so superior to anything I ever knew before that I have no desire to go back. I became clear on who I wanted to be, and that has been a powerful influence on readiness to take the next step, number three.

3. Then "Behold" Those Things That Will Get Us There: Romans 12:1–2 is one of the great set of super-verses in Scripture. It tells us to choose what we want to become, and then **behold the things that will get us there**:

> Therefore I urge you, brethren, by the mercies of God, to present your bodies a living and holy sacrifice, acceptable to God, *which is* your spiritual service of worship. And do not be conformed to this world, but be transformed by the renewing of your mind, so that you may prove what the will of God is, that which is good and acceptable and perfect.

When we work this passage backward, we see that in order for our lives to be living proof that the will of God is good and acceptable and perfect, we must be transformed, and if we are to be transformed, we must have our minds renewed.

It is all there—the whole idea in a nutshell.

So, to renew your mind, you must behold things that will get you *The "How"* to become the person you have chosen to become. Obviously, you must also not behold those things that do not get you where you want to go. It is really that simple, and when you embrace that principle, it answers many of the seemingly tricky questions in life.

Resist temptation to behold things that will take you away from your goal, knowing that they only pollute your integrity and retard your progress toward your goal.

This, of course, is where the challenge of electronic communication is so problematic. It is so pervasive, and for so much of it, the best we behold is neutral, and the worst takes us away from God. We end up beholding things that will not get us where we want to go. This is a huge principle—so huge that it will take other chapters to unpack it. In this chapter, we just make the point clearly: we become what we behold, and if we indiscriminately behold the message of much electronic media, we will be captured by modern culture.

Conclusion

When I was in college, Francis Schaeffer, a noted American theologian and philosopher of the time, wrote that people get their values the same way they get the measles—by being around others who have them.[6] As a result, many people end up with values, which, upon further reflection, they might have chosen to avoid. This hit me with thunderous impact because it was the first time I remember seeing my life objectively. For the first time, I was able to step outside myself and look at my life, almost as a third party. For the first time, I saw that I had caught my values the same way I caught the measles. And I decided then and there I would change and would choose my values rather than letting my values choose me.

. . . people get their values the same way they get the measles—by being around others who have them.

Some yes; Some are definitely culturally influenced

Are the values you have the ones that you would really like to have? Or would you like to have different, better values? Would you like to be better, more than you are?

The thought occurred to me, *What would I be like if I had been born into a different environment? What if, instead of being born into a family of*

18

*modest means and education in a rural part of Indiana, I had been born into
an affluent, highly educated family in Boston? Or into a blue-blooded family with a military background in Charleston, South Carolina? Or a politi-
cally powerful family in Southern California? Would I be different than I
am now?* Absolutely. I would have been in a family and an environment that would have created significantly different attitudes, habits,
and values than the ones I grew up with.

Then, I was struck with a profoundly liberating idea. I could
become who I wanted to be. I could not undo history, I could not erase
my heritage, and I could not change the past, but I did not have to be
a slave to them. I could choose to become the person I wanted to be.
Specifically, I could choose my attitudes, values, and behavior—and I
could begin to work on my limitations and capitalize on my strengths.

If I thought I would be a better person for keeping helpful characteristics I grew up with, of which there were many, I could do so. If I
would be a better person for shedding some of my limiting characteristics and adopting some more helpful characteristics, I could do that.
I decided that I was no longer going to be a cork floating down the
stream of life, that I was going to choose who I was going to become.
It has been many years since, and that decision has made all the
difference.

We all have that choice, and it is never too soon or too late to
make it. In fact, it is better than that, because Scripture informs us as
to what we should be like, and the Holy Spirit will help us get there.
But we must do three things in the process.

1. We must realize that we become what we behold.

2. We must choose what we want to become.

3. We must behold the things that will get us there.

Summary

Electronic media is powerful and pervasive and is radically shaping modern culture with profoundly secular attitudes, values, and behavior. Because we become what we behold, if we are not to be swept away from biblical attitudes, values, and behavior into secular ones, we must choose what we want to become and behold the things that will get us there. Then and only then will we have the personal capacity and moral authority to disciple people into a level of spiritual maturity that will enable them to escape the hold of modern culture themselves.

Review for Memory

1. We must realize that we b_ecome_ what we b_ehold_.
   (Page 12)

2. Therefore, we must c_hoose_ what we want to become.
   (Page 15)

3. We must b_ehold_ the things that will get us there.
   (Page 17)

4. Two critical questions we must ask ourselves are:
   a. What do you w_ant_ out of life?
   b. Are you willing to pay the p_rice_? (Page 15)

Review for Understanding

Summarize this chapter in fifty words or less:

We become what we behold, but we get a say in who we want to become. Then, it is simply a matter of paying the price to behold the things that will equip me to be that person.

_____

_____

_____

_____

_____

_____

Review for Application

Write out what you want out of life.

- Abiding, soul-satisfying intimacy w/ Jesus — to really know Him as my closest companion. To hear His voice.
- Life-giving, refining relationships.
- Adventures and huge answered prayers w/ Jesus.
- To be a woman who radiates Jesus, loves and sees others well, is humble + peace + joy-filled
- To see + aid in building Kingdom in the U.S + abroad on a path only God could pave.

Are you willing to pay the price?

Yes ✓ No ___

Why or why not?

Because its worth it — everything else pales in comparison.

CHAPTER 3

Central Passage: "For all that is in the world, the lust of the flesh and the lust of the eyes and the boastful pride of life, is not from the Father, but is from the world" (1 John 2:16).

Modern Culture Requires a Holistic Discipleship Strategy

Cultural opposition to Christianity places historic demands on our discipleship strategy requiring that we target each of a Christian's seven spiritual responsibilities.

Culture is a powerful thing. A story is commonly told of an experiment in which five hungry monkeys were placed in an empty cage with a ladder in the middle. At the top of the ladder was a bunch of bananas. When one of the monkeys began to climb the ladder, it was sprayed with cold water, preventing it from getting to the bananas. However, not only was that monkey sprayed, but all the monkeys were sprayed with cold water. Later, when a second monkey attempted to climb the ladder, again, it was sprayed, along with all the other monkeys. This went on until none of the monkeys would climb the ladder for fear of getting sprayed with cold water.

Then, as the story goes, one of the wet monkeys was taken out and a new monkey was put in the cage. When it started to climb the ladder, the other four monkeys, fearing they would be sprayed, grabbed the new monkey and prevented it from climbing the ladder. This went on until the new monkey learned not to climb the ladder. Then, they took out a second monkey that had been sprayed and put in a new one that had not, and the process started over again. The new monkey started to climb the ladder, the other four prevented it until it, too, learned not to climb the ladder.

This continued until there were no longer any monkeys in the cage that had been sprayed with water, but when a new monkey was introduced to the cage and started up the ladder, the other four monkeys prevented the newest monkey from climbing the ladder. They did not know why, they just knew not to climb the ladder, even if they were hungry.[1]

This story provides an effective parable for the power of culture. Culture is a powerful, almost living thing, and every societal institution has a culture, which all people in it tend to conform to. By our very nature, we all tend to follow the attitudes, values, and behavior of those around us. This helps us if the culture around us is biblical. It hurts us if it is not.

The Limitations of Twentieth-Century Discipleship Models

The United States, in the last fifty years, has provided an almost clinical study of the power of culture to help or hurt alignment with biblical principles. As was stated in the introduction, if you conformed to popular culture in the United States in 1950, you did not violate any of the Ten Commandments. Today if you conform to popular culture, you violate many of the Ten Commandments.

This affects not only American culture at large but also the church in America because everyone who is part of the church in America is also part of larger American culture. Because of this, the attitudes, values, and behavior of Christians have evolved, so that today when polls are taken, older generations tend to be more conservative than younger generations who tend to evolve with the culture.

In addition to the typical devolution of belief and behavior in younger generations, the further shortcomings of American discipleship processes are reflected by what Christian pollster George Barna calls the "the determined, readily discernible theological ignorance of Christians." He describes the church as being fairly astute in some areas of knowledge and "embarrassingly ignorant" in others. This condition is attributable to Christian education processes which he describes as "asystematic" (not systematic).[2]

The Problem

So, we have a two-edged sword. On the one edge we have predictable weakening of biblical belief and behavior that is common simply because younger generations tend to devolve in belief and behavior from their older counterparts. And, on the other edge, we have an entrenched, asystematic education process that further contributes to a weakening of Christian behavior and belief.

Discipleship strategies conceived in the twentieth century, or built on twentieth-century assumptions, tend to be partial strategies.

Therefore, a discipleship strategy that is adequate for the demands of the church in America in the twenty-first century must be like filling a cube with sand. It must get out to all four corners at the bottom of the cube (basic learning) and then must progress to the top (advanced learning), keeping out to all four corners as it rises, not leaving anything out.

Discipleship strategies conceived in the twentieth century, or built on twentieth-century assumptions, tend to be partial strategies. Some focus on what a disciple should know. Others focus on how disciples should live. Still others focus on what disciples should do. They tend not to be holistic, including everything a Christian needs to know, be, and do to be a complete Christian, moving comprehensively from the basic to the advanced.

While we cannot know if it is correct, as I suggested in the introduction, my assumption is that those discipleship strategies were conceived in a time when culture in America tended to support biblical truth and values. As a result, society as a whole tended to know biblical truth and conform to biblical behavior, even if given individuals were not true Christians.

This allowed disciplers to pick and choose the greatest perceived needs in discipleship, focus on those, and assume the rest—a foundational level of knowledge and behavior. Said another way, discipleship systems could focus on the greatest perceived needs of mature Christian belief and behavior and count on American culture to fill in the rest. The fact is, that seemed to be a reasonable approach at the time. Why try to disciple people into a level of belief and behavior that they already had as a result of being an American? Rather, one could just assume the foundational belief and behavior and polish off the disciple by adding what was missing.

The Requirements of Twenty-First-Century Discipleship Models

Time has radically changed that, however. Today, not only can we not count on American culture to fill in the gaps in our discipleship system with biblical belief and behavior, but also we must assume culture will fill in any gaps in our discipleship system with unbiblical belief and behavior.

As a result of the fact that modern culture makes nearly all things worse, an essential feature of a Brave New Discipleship system that is adequate to the demands of our Brave New World is that it must be holistic. It must be complete. It must get out to all four corners of the Christian life, assuming nothing from culture and society except hostility and opposition. Addressing the complete needs of the disciple has not been a characteristic of the past. It must be a characteristic of the future. Otherwise, a discipleship system for the future, if it is going to impact a broad segment of the church, is doomed.

Therefore, while it might not seem radical on the surface, **to create a discipleship system that assumes responsibility for every facet of spiritual growth is essential if we are going to meet the life-demands of the twenty-first century**.

The Seven Marks of a Complete Discipleship Strategy

To that end, let me tell you my story. Years ago, I sat in a seminary classroom listening to master teacher Dr. Hendricks expound on a passage that few of us even knew was in the Bible: Ezra 7:10, which says, "For Ezra had set his heart to study the law of the Lord, and to practice *it*, and to teach *His* statutes and ordinances in Israel." Dr. Hendricks taught that Ezra studied the law of the Lord to acquire a biblical knowledge base. He practiced it to develop a biblical lifestyle, and he taught it to fulfill a biblical ministry. **In Dr. Hendricks's words, this was the "know-be-do" principle.**

Then he said a person's lifestyle will never go beyond his knowledge, and a person's ministry will never go beyond his lifestyle. A mature Christian is a complete package.

For a brief moment, the world stopped rotating. I sat there transfixed as one of the most important things I had heard in all my life lodged permanently in my heart and mind. I had never seen this truth before; and yet, as soon as I heard it, it seemed obviously, blindingly true. I knew of people who knew a lot but who were not mature in their character. I knew people who were busy doing things but did not know anything. I had been both and was in seminary to try to correct my condition.

> . . . a person's lifestyle will never go beyond his knowledge, and a person's ministry will never go beyond his lifestyle.

Up until that point, figuring out the Christian life for me was trial and error, hit and miss, like trying to build a house without a blueprint. That day, I instinctively understood that the gigantic truth in Ezra 7:10—the know-be-do principle—was a key part of the spiritual blueprint.

A year or two later, another life-defining moment happened that intensified my desire for a spiritual blueprint. As a freshly scrubbed seminary graduate teaching in a Christian college, I led a young man to Christ. When he finished praying, he looked at me in innocence and asked simply, "Now what?"

It is commonly said that when you have a close brush with death, your whole past flashes in front of you. Instead, my whole future flashed in front on me. I knew I did not know the answer to that question, and because I was in the ministry, my whole future depended on knowing the answer. I knew bits of the answer, of course. I knew to tell him to read his Bible and pray and go to church—things like that. But in terms of giving him a comprehensive blueprint for the Christian life, I could not do it, and it rocked my world. I thought, I need to know the whole answer to that question, and I dedicated myself to trying to figure it out. I knew that Ezra 7:10 was a key, though intuitively, I also knew it was not everything.

For decades I have studied that issue, and I have come to believe that, when you boil it all down to its irreducible minimum, there are three major responsibilities of a complete Christian. **A complete Christian is one who:**

a. **Worships God**

b. **Grows spiritually**

c. **Impacts his world**

This covers God, self, and others. There are not any other responsibilities. Everything a Christian is supposed to do fits under one of those three categories.

However, while this triad is accurate, those three categories are so super-condensed it was helpful for me to expand them one level, like a pull-down menu on a computer screen. Otherwise, it was too easy to overlook a key responsibility. For example, while Christians are to worship, it is helpful to understand that we are to worship individually as well as corporately. Because people tend to see one or the other of these two responsibilities more clearly, we have to focus on both so we do not neglect one.

The same is true with our second responsibility—growth. While it is true that we are all to grow, it is helpful to know that we are to grow in three areas—and this is where the know-be-do principle from Ezra applies—our biblical knowledge (know), our Christlike lifestyle (be), and our ministry skill (do). A person also tends to see one of these three more clearly than the other two. So, if we are to avoid neglecting any of these growth areas, we have to keep all three on the radar screen.

Finally, while it is true we are to impact our world, it is helpful to understand that doing so includes impacting both the church as well as the non-church world. Again, Christians tend to see one of these responsibilities more clearly than the other. To make sure we do not neglect one, we need to focus on both.

So, the three overall responsibilities of a complete Christian—to worship, to grow, and to impact—are best understood in their expanded form of seven. In this form, the complete Christian is one who:

1. Worships God individually

2. Worships God corporately

3. Grows in biblical knowledge

4. Grows in Christlike lifestyle

5. Grows in ministry skill

6. Impacts the church

7. Impacts the world

These, then, are the seven marks of a complete Christian: **A complete Christian is one who worships God individually, worships God corporately, grows in biblical knowledge, grows in Christlike lifestyle, grows in ministry skill, and impacts the church and the world**. Understanding these seven marks is a guiding beacon for the Christian life. It enables us to see the whole so that we do not leave out any of the parts in our Christian experience. We must focus on all seven responsibilities simultaneously to avoid having holes in our Christian life.

If we focus on all seven marks, we get out to all four corners of the cube of discipleship. And if we move from the basic to the advanced, we will fill up the discipleship cube effectively, giving many Christians a chance to mature deeply because of what the church is doing rather than a few doing so in spite of what the church is doing, to echo Dallas Willard's observation from chapter 1. This is a biblical foundation undergirding a system that is adequate for discipleship in the twenty-first century. For the next seven chapters, we will look at each of these seven marks of a complete Christian, after which we will look at methods, technology, and approaches that are necessary to effectively implement this biblical foundation. Without this, we will not be able to create a discipleship system that will stand up to the demands of an otherwise terrifying and spiritually dangerous world we are entering.

We must focus on all seven responsibilities simultaneously to avoid having holes in our Christian life.

Review for Memory

1. To create a discipleship system that assumes responsibility for e _very_ f _acet_ of spiritual growth is essential if we are going to meet the life-demands of the twenty-first century. (Page 27)

2. Ezra 7:10 describes the k_now_ - b_e_ - d_o_ principle. (Page 27)

3. A complete Christian is one who:
   a. W_orships_ God
   b. G_rows_ spiritually
   c. I_mpacts_ the world (Page 28)

4. These three principles are so super-condensed that it is helpful to expand them into seven:
   a. Worships i_ndividually_
   b. Worships c_orporately_
   c. Grows in b_iblical_ k_nowledge_
   d. Grows in c_hristlike_ l_ifestyle_
   e. Grows in m_inistry_ s_kill_
   f. Impacts the c_church_
   g. Impacts the w_orld_ (Page 30)

Review for Understanding

Summarize the paragraph on pages 26–27, beginning with "As a result of the fact that modern culture makes nearly all things worse" in twenty-five words or less:

_____

_____

_____

_____

_____

_____

_____

Review for Application

Write out how you think that knowing the information in this chapter will change your discipleship approach:

_____

_____

_____

_____

_____

_____

_____

Central Passage: "God is spirit, and those who worship Him must worship in spirit and truth" (John 4:24).

Mark No. 1: A Complete Christian Worships God Individually

A rich Christian experience requires a vital inner life. Therefore, the complete Christian cultivates his inner life, setting aside some time each day for individual worship, praying, and meditating throughout the day and dedicating each activity as an act of worship to God.

The mind is the battlefield on which the Christian life is **won or lost.** If the Christian wins that battle, a vibrant Christian experience can be his. If the Christian loses that battle, he sinks to a life of ineffectiveness and defeat. It is impossible to overstate the importance of this challenge. Therefore, the twenty-first-century Christian must understand the power of governing the mind and the consequences for not governing the mind.

battle of the mind!

The power of the mind has been demonstrated in unusual and dramatic ways. In research at Harvard University, Tibetan monks demonstrated an extraordinary capacity to lower their metabolism, breathing rate, heart rate, and blood pressure with their minds. In an even more dramatic display, a monk was able, through meditation, to raise his body heat dramatically. While he was sitting in a room in which the temperature was forty degrees (the same as a refrigerator), sheets soaked in cold water were placed over his shoulders. Normally this would produce uncontrolled shivering, and possibly eventual death. However, he was able to raise his body heat so high that before long, steam began rising from the sheets. They dried in about an hour. The meditator was unaffected.[1]

. . . the mind is a remarkable instrument that has under-appreciated and under-utilized capacity.

Of course, the meditation philosophy of Buddhist monks is not compatible with Christianity, and so this example should not be understood as recommending Buddhist meditation practices. It is simply intended to point out that the mind is a remarkable instrument that has underappreciated and underutilized capacity.

The power of the mind has also been demonstrated in the experiences of prisoners of war. Studies have been conducted to try to determine why some prisoners of war survive their experience with relatively little permanent psychological and emotional damage, while others are debilitated by it. What was learned was that some prisoners of war go into an elaborate inner world in order to survive. In Vietnam, for example, the outer world of the American prisoners of war was so horrifying, so inhumane, and so meaningless that to survive they had to escape into an inner world that they created mentally. The ones who survived the best were the ones who most effectively used their imagination to construct a vivid inner world to occupy their minds and protect their emotions.

In his book *Faith of My Fathers*, John McCain recounts his experience as a POW in Vietnam. He writes that of all the forms of torture, solitary confinement is the worst. It crushes the spirit and weakens resistance more effectively than any other form of mistreatment.

> The onset of despair is immediate, and it is a formidable foe. You have to fight it with any means necessary. I devised memory games to keep my faculties sound. For days I tried to remember the names of all the pilots in my squadron and our sister squadron. I also prayed more often and more fervently that I ever had as a free man.
>
> Many prisoners spent their hours exercising their minds by concentrating on an academic discipline or hobby they were proficient in. I knew men who mentally designed buildings and airplanes. I knew others who spent days and weeks working out complicated math formulas. I reconstructed from memory books and movies I once enjoyed. I tried to compose books and plays of my own, often acting out sequences in the quiet solitude of my cell.[2]

Stories are commonly circulated of other examples of this kind of cultivation of the inner world. Reportedly, one soldier from the Midwest mentally built a house in such detail that he could discuss with his cellmate the color of tile on the bathroom floor off the master bedroom, and later built that house exactly as he had imagined it in his mind.[3] Another soldier was said to have carefully scratched out a piano keyboard on the cement floor of his cell and imagined playing a piano for hours a day, envisioning in detail which fingers were needed to hit which keys and how hard to hit them, to play songs he had memorized before his incarceration. He even composed new songs while in prison and was able to play them from memory on a real piano when he returned home, even though he had never actually heard them before. Yet another soldier was said to have mentally played golf courses he had memorized. He imagined in exact detail which course he was on, seeing in his mind's eye each tee, each fairway, each bunker, each green, and mentally rehearsing each shot. He envisioned where the ball went, made the next shot, chipped to the green, one-putted (of course), and then moved on to the next hole. In this story, he reported being a better golfer after his experience as a POW than he was before.

Whether or not these stories are accurate in every detail, they are illustrative of the type of mental exercises that McCain and others engaged in to develop the ability to survive in their seen world by mentally cultivating their unseen world.

Christians have a similar challenge! The physical world in which we live is so foreign and hostile to biblical values that if we are going to prosper spiritually, we must create an inner spiritual world to which we retreat, drawing on the reality of that spiritual world for the capacity to live well in the physical world. Almost like prisoners of war, we must spend large amounts of time mentally blocking out the physical world, magnifying the spiritual world, cultivating our awareness of biblical truth, feeding our understanding of biblical values, and mentally rehearsing biblical behavior so that when we live in the physical world, we will think and act according to heaven's values and not earth's.

The prisoners of war and the Buddhist monks demonstrate that the mind is a powerful thing, that it is underappreciated and underutilized. If we want to achieve our potential as servants of Christ, if we want the power to withstand the corrosive and corrupting influence of modern culture, we must rise to the challenge of loving God with all our mind, dedicating our mind fully to the service of Christ.

This is, of course, extremely difficult. It is the very battleground of life. But the freedom to have a rich Christian experience depends on rising to this considerable challenge. Realizing the untapped power of the God-given gift of our mind, we must learn greater ways to use the mind to deepen our relationship with the Lord and strengthen our walk with Him.

One reason this is so difficult, as we have already seen, is that we tend, by nature, to conform to culture around us. We tend to become like the people we grow up around. This is why deep southerners are different from upper northeasterners and why Germans are different from Chinese or Greeks.

As we conform to the world around us, we naturally conform in many ways to things that are not Christian. This world tells us that we only go around once in life, so we must grab all the pleasure we can. This world tells us that success in life depends on the things we own, our achievements, and the way we look. This world tells us that pleasure in life is physical and emotional and that we need to please our body and feelings. Because of the pervasiveness of this message in American culture, it is only natural that people absorb these values, yet these values collide with biblical truth.

Contrary to those values, Scripture tells us that this life is not ultimate reality. Scripture tells us that ultimate fulfillment in this life is not physical and emotional, but spiritual. Scripture tells us that we go around twice—once in this short world and again in an eternal world—and that rather than to feed the pleasures of this life, we should invest in the pleasures of the next life. We need to understand the difference between the two and live for the things that will matter in the long run.

This idea is captured brilliantly by journalist and author Peggy Noonan, again in *Life, Liberty and the Pursuit of Happiness*:

> Our ancestors believed in two worlds, and understood this to be the solitary, poor, nasty, brutish and short one. We are the first generation of man that actually expected to find happiness here on earth, and our search for it has caused such unhappiness. The reason: if you do not believe in another, higher world, if you believe only in the flat material world around you, if you believe that this is your only chance at happiness—if that is what you believe, then you are more than disappointed when the world does not give you a good measure of its riches, you are in despair.[4]

Christians can fall prey to this despair just as non-Christians, if they are living for the same things non-Christians are living for— if they buy the false values of the world. And, buy them they will if they do not take steps to offset them. Freedom from the values (and troubles) of the world depends on slavery to the values (and blessings) of Christian truth.

As the proverb goes, "if you want to be free to sail the seven seas, you must make yourself a slave to the compass." This is true in all areas of life. Every bondage has a corresponding freedom, and every freedom has a corresponding bondage. For example, you can be a slave to the toothbrush and free from cavities, or you can be free from the toothbrush and a slave to cavities. But you cannot be free from the toothbrush and free from cavities. That kind of absolute freedom does not exist, because all of our actions have consequences. Therefore, one of the great issues of life is to choose carefully your freedoms, for from them come your bondages, and to choose carefully your bondages because from them come your freedoms. This is especially true in the Christian life. If Christians want a rich spiritual experience based on a vital inner life, it requires a corresponding bondage to the spiritual disciplines that yield spiritual freedom.

Every bondage has a corresponding freedom, and every freedom has a corresponding bondage.

That is so Good

Yet the values of modern popular culture do not include self-discipline, self-sacrifice, and self-direction. As a result, modern American culture is increasingly shallow and empty with little concern for the inner life. Therefore, American Christians as a whole tend to be shallower, weaker, smaller, and emptier for it. If we want to escape being shallow, weak, small, and empty, we must cultivate an inner life, nurture our daily walk with God, and commit ourselves to living transformed outer lives by the power of a transformed inner life.

The apostle Paul made this point clearly in 2 Corinthians 4:16–18, when he wrote:

> Therefore we do not lose heart, but though our outer man is decaying, yet our inner man is being renewed day by day. For momentary, light affliction is producing for us an eternal weight of glory far beyond all comparison, while we look not at the things which are seen, but at the things which are not seen; for the things which are seen are temporal, but the things which are not seen are eternal.

This passage challenges us not to live according to the attitudes, values, and behavior of the physical world around us, but to renew our minds so that we live according to the spiritual world to which God has called us. Further, in Colossians 3, Paul encourages us to "keep seeking the things above, where Christ is, seated at the right hand of God. Set your mind on the things above, not on the things that are on earth" (vv. 1–2).

Joe Stowell, in his book *Eternity*, told a compelling story of professional golfer Paul Azinger, whom the Lord—in an act of His severe mercy—brought to a stark awareness of this foundational Christian truth:

> Paul Azinger was at the height of his professional golf career when a doctor told him he had life-threatening cancer. Up to that moment he had not given much thought to dying. Life was too all-consuming for him to stop and consider the reality of the grave and all that is beyond. But that encounter with the inevitability of eternity was an abrupt reality check. His life would never again be the same. Even the $1.4 million he had made as a professional golfer that year paled to insignificance. All he could think about was what the chaplain of the tour had said: "We think that we are in the land of the living going to the land of the dying, when in reality, we are in the land of the dying headed for the land of the living."[5]

Embracing the reality of the world to come radically alters everything in this world. Our values are prioritized and purified. Money, things, time, friends, enemies, family, and life itself are adjusted and given their appropriate worth and place.

As we live each day embracing the attitudes, values, and behavior of the next world, we find ourselves getting more and more out of step with the physical world and more and more in step with the world to which God calls us. It is an immense challenge! We must spend sufficient mental time in the spiritual world, so that we may live successfully in the physical world that is hostile to us. We will not have a normal or deeply satisfying Christian experience until we master this challenge.

Jesus is our great example for this principle. He worked hard at nurturing His inner life. Luke 5:16 tells us that Jesus "would *often* slip away to the wilderness and pray." He sometimes prayed all night (Luke 6:12) and would retreat to solitude during challenging times (John 6:15). If Jesus worked hard at nurturing His inner life, how much more must we work at nurturing our inner life?

Drawing on this characteristic of Jesus, Dallas Willard, in his book *The Spirit of the Disciplines***, made the point that we cannot behave "on the spot" as Jesus did unless we live the way Jesus did before the "spot" got there.** He made the point that it is futile to try to imitate Jesus in the difficult moments of life unless we adopt Jesus' overall lifestyle.[6] What He did when He was alone is what enabled Him to respond with spiritual success in the small and great moments of His life. The same must be true of us.

In athletics, the gravity-defying dunks, the blazing speed of touchdown runs, the furious swings of bats that send balls over the wall are a result not of spontaneous effort but of heart-pounding, backbreaking, muscle-aching, and time-consuming preparation. The glory of the spectacular play is but the tip of the iceberg of sometimes lonely, boring, painful, and exacting preparation.

Willard makes the point with young boys who want to be great baseball players but do not want to practice.[7] They want to run, hit, and pitch as well as their major-league idol, and so they use the mitt that idol has autographed and the bat that he endorsed and wear a jersey with his number. They hold the bat the way he does and slide into second base headfirst the way he does. But it does not work, because those are not the things that made the hero great. The star performer got great by everything he did before the game started.

In his book *The Life God Blesses*, Gordon MacDonald writes:

> Another thing that makes spirituality a rare commodity . . . is the fact that it is often forged in the context of silence and submission, two experiences that most of us have been taught to avoid whenever possible. The almost demonic spirit of noise that has filled the air about our lives is a surefire guarantee that most people will never inquire of their souls.[8]

This is why demonic attack is so different here than in Africa, Asia, etc.

But inquire of our souls we must if we are to have a vital inner life! **We must find the resolve to spend enough time cultivating our inner world that we will be able to offset the influence of the outer world.**

It is in the cultivation of our inner life that spiritual transformation and spiritual power take root in our hearts and bear fruit in our lives. In personal worship, we express our love to God, we praise Him for His character and His loving actions. We honor Him in our hearts and minds as David did in the Psalms, not as skillfully, but hopefully as sincerely. Beyond that, **the purpose of individual worship is to feed our inner lives so that we will be able to live well in our outer lives.**

Review for Memory

1. The mind is the b *attlefield* _____ on which the Christian life is won or lost. (Page 33)

2. We tend, by nature, to conform to c *ulture* _____ around us. (Page 36)

3. We must find the resolve to spend enough time cultivating our
i _inner_ world that we will be able to offset the influence of the o _uter_ world. (Page 41)

4. Dallas Willard: We cannot behave "on the spot" as Jesus did
unless we l _ive_ the way Jesus did before the "spot"
got there. (Page 40)

5. The goal of individual worship is to f _eed_ our inner lives
so that we will be able to l _ive_ w _ell_ in our
outer lives. (Page 41)

Review for Understanding

Summarize in one paragraph what you think the most important
message of this chapter is:

_Due to the ease with which we conform to the culture
around us, and the fact that said culture is very
opposite Christianity, we must prioritize cultivating
our inner spiritual life. It is our mind that determines
our actions. We must be intentional to discipline
our thoughts to focus on heavenly things. These
are eternal and bring true joy. Culture would
have us focus only on the present._

Review for Application

Write out how you think that knowing this will influence your habits of individual worship:

I loved the quote about choosing your freedoms and choosing your bondage. I really want to choose the bondage of the disciplines - solitude, silence, rule of life - in order to experience greater freedom in Jesus. I want to stop being so free with my phone/media usage.

Central Passage: *"Let us consider how to stimulate one another to love and good deeds, not forsaking our own assembling together" (Heb. 10:24–25).*

Mark No. 2: A Complete Christian Worships God Corporately

The Christian life was never meant to be lived alone. Therefore, a complete Christian worships God with other Christians and integrates his entire life with other Christians.

The 1968 movie *2001: A Space Odyssey,*[1] is a sci-fi masterpiece imagining, from that vantage point many years ago, what life might be like at the turn of the twenty-first century. Much of the action takes place on an orbiting space station high above the earth. In one harrowing scene, an astronaut gets disconnected from the space station during a space walk and begins floating silently away into the eternal darkness surrounding him. No one knows he is outside the station, so there is no hope of rescue. The image is of a human being floating away from all other human beings into absolute blackness and solitude, left utterly alone to die. It would be one of the most terrifying ways to die.

That scene was crafted specifically by the producers of the film to make a statement about humanity—that if we are not careful to manage technology and continue to value relationships above technology, humanity will drift away into terrifying aloneness.

The reason that scene is so horrifying is that we are not created to be alone. We are created to be part of a larger whole. We are created to live our lives in harmony and relationship with others. This is true of all humans but especially of Christians, who have not only the connection of human nature with one another but also the connection of being fellow members of the body of Christ.

> We are created to be part of a larger whole. We are created to live our lives in harmony and relationship with others.

We were created by God to be Three Musketeers not Lone Rangers. The motto of the Three Musketeers was "One for all, and all for one." That sums up the Christian ideal pretty well. **Humans are social beings because God is a social being, and we are created in God's image.** Therefore, our highest good is realized as we live as God lives, in harmony and community with others.

Because of human defects and limitations, it can be easier said than done. I once heard the story of a man who had been shipwrecked on a desert island for six years. For the entire 2,190 days, he never saw another human being. So when a cruise ship happened to anchor nearby and send a party ashore, he was beside himself with joy. At last, he was with people again.

The captain of the ship looked up on the crest of the hill on the island behind them and saw three straw huts stretched along the skyline. He asked the castaway what the three huts were.

The castaway beamed. "Well, the first one is my church," he said with pride. "That's where I worship. And the middle one is my house. That's where I live."

The captain asked, "Well, what's that third hut over there?"

A dark cloud crossed the castaway's face momentarily as he replied, "Oh. That's the church I used to go to."

We smile, and yet it is only funny because it contains a seed of truth. Getting along with other Christians can be so hard that sometimes, if we had to get along with ourselves, we could not do it. But part of living a complete Christian life is living in unity and harmony with other Christians, especially worshiping with them. Someone once said that the church is like Noah and his family inside the ark with all those animals during the flood. If it were not for the storm on the outside, they could not have stood the stench on the inside.

This is not unique to our time. The New Testament is filled with letters to churches that had problems—in some cases, big problems. People were living in sin, individuals were fighting with one another, groups were breaking up into factions. There are not any root problems in the church today that we do not see in the New Testament. While that may be reassuring on one level, on another level, it does not make our church experience any easier.

Yet, difficult as other Christians can sometimes be, and disappointing as the church experience can sometimes be, corporate worship is something that all God's children need to care about. C. S. Lewis wrote, "The New Testament does not envision a solitary religion; some kind of regular assembly for worship and instruction is everywhere taken for granted in the Epistles. So we must be regular practicing members of the church."[2] Lewis came to this conclusion unwillingly. In *God in the Dock*, he wrote of the process:

> When I first became a Christian . . . I thought that I could do it on my own, by retiring to my rooms and reading theology, and I wouldn't go to the churches . . . I disliked very much their hymns, which I considered to be fifth-rate poems set to sixth-rate music. But as I went, I saw the great merit of it. I realized that the hymns were being sung with devotion and benefit by an old saint in elastic-side

boots in the opposite pew, and then you realize that you aren't fit to clean those boots.[3]

So, it would seem Lewis came kicking and struggling into the church, just as he had come earlier in his life—as he described it—kicking and struggling into Christianity, asserting that in spite of all the imperfections of the church, we are to join it and help make it better.[4]

God is a social being. He is a Trinity. He is three, yet one. The unity that the Father, Son, and Holy Spirit experience within the Godhead is one of the great characteristics of our God. And we are created in His image. He wants us to live in unity, in oneness with Him and with one another. It is the highest good that we can experience.

Christians Gather for Two Reasons

As Christians, we gather to worship for two reasons. First is to call public attention to the greatness of who God is and what He has done. In the great worship experience described in Revelation 4:11, we see the worshipers saying, "Worthy are You, our Lord and our God, to receive glory and honor and power; for You created all things, and because of Your will they existed, and were created." Later they say, "Worthy is the Lamb that was slain to receive power and riches and wisdom and might and honor and glory and blessing" (5:12). And "to Him who sits on the throne, and to the Lamb, be blessing and honor and glory and dominion forever and ever" (v. 13).

Indeed, the first great purpose for worship is to call public attention to the greatness of who God is and what He has done.

The second purpose is to encourage one another to love and good deeds. The writer of the book of Hebrews said, "Let us consider how to stimulate one another to love and good deeds, not forsaking our own assembling together, as is the habit of some" (10:24–25). The books of the New Testament assume believers will be united with a local spiritual fellowship and worshiping together.

▶ 1 Corinthians 1:2 is written to the church of God at Corinth, as are many of the epistles. It was assumed that the way to communicate with Christians was to communicate to the local church, which gathered for such purposes.

▶ 1 Corinthians 11:18: "When you come together as a church, I hear that divisions exist among you." The Corinthian church was in the habit of coming together.

▶ In 1 Corinthians 16:2, we have the record of Christians taking up an offering on the first day of the week, the day they were gathered to worship.

▶ Colossians 4:16 says, "When this letter is read among you, have it also read in the church of the Laodiceans," which assumes those churches gathered for corporate services.

▶ The book of 1 Timothy was written to instruct the church in Ephesus on how to conduct themselves in corporate worship services, as was a segment of 1 Corinthians (chapters 12–14).

▶ In verse 2 of Philemon, Paul sends greetings "to Apphia our sister, and to Archippus our fellow soldier, and to the church in your house."

Repeating what Lewis said, "Some kind of regular assembly for worship and instruction is everywhere taken for granted in the Epistles."

Can you imagine next Sunday, showing up at a church and your being the only one there? The door is unlocked, the sanctuary is a comfortable temperature, the lights are on, but you are the only one in the pews. You read Scripture, you sing songs, you leave money for an offering, and you take communion. You do the things that you would do in a normal worship service. But would you like that? Would it be the same as when you gather with all the other people who are normally there?

Something important, something valuable, and something higher happens when we gather to worship with others than when we worship God alone. God created us as social beings, to be part of one another, to join with others on a higher and greater plane for corporate worship. He calls Christians to spiritual unity, which assumes a commitment to corporate worship. The picture we see in Scripture of Christians is that we are members of a spiritual body; we are living stones in a spiritual building, and our corporate nature is to be expressed in corporate worship.

Many of us have the idea that it is the church's responsibility to put on a good show for us that we enjoy and that moves us emotionally. We see the ministers, the special music, the singers, and instrumentalists as the actors on a stage—with ourselves as the audience. If the show is good, we reward the actors with our approval, our presence, and maybe even our financial support. If the show is not so good, we reduce our response. We want God to come down and bless us—reward us—for getting out of bed and worshiping Him.

True worship, however, is the responsibility of each person in the pew. When worship is understood correctly, each person in the pew is one of the actors while the ministers, singers, musicians, and others are merely prompters for us. God Himself is the audience. Rather than our evaluating the minister's professional skills, God is evaluating our sincerity. That is worship.

James Packer, in his book *God Has Spoken*, wrote:

> God's purpose in revelation is to make friends with us. It was to this end that He created us rational beings, bearing His image, able to think and hear and speak and love; He wanted there to be genuine personal affection and friendship, two-sided, between Himself and us—a relationship, not like that between man and his dog, but like that of a father to his son, or a husband to his wife. Loving friendship between two persons has no ulterior motive; it is an end in itself. And that is God's end in revelation. He speaks to us simply to fulfill the purpose for which we were made; that is, to bring into

being a relationship in which He is a friend to us, and we to Him, He finding His joy in giving us gifts, and we finding ours in giving Him thanks.[5]

That is the point and purpose of worship. God deeply values our worship.

Christians are to live their entire lives in relationship and harmony with other Christians. If you have ever spent any time tending a fire, you know that two coals by themselves will go out. But if you put them together, they will burn brightly. So it is with Christians. Separate them, and they go out. Put them together, and they burn brightly. If you do not attend church regularly, if you do not integrate your life with other Christians, you will lose your ability to consistently think Christianly and to act Christianly. Without the input of sermons, worship services, fellowship with other Christians, and the consistent input of other Christians into your life, you gradually forget who you are (you are a child of God) and how you are to act (you are to act like Jesus would if He were in your shoes).

More than just attending services on Sunday mornings, integrate your life with other Christians. You are part of this living, spiritual organism called the church, and you are cut off from your lifeline and your destiny if you do not integrate your life with the lives of other Christians. You are like an arm or a leg lying off to the side of the rest of the body. It is not normal or healthy for you to be alone. We shrivel, we get distorted, and we become unbalanced and misdirected unless we are part of a community of other believers.

In Ephesians 4:15–16 Paul wrote:

> Speaking the truth in love, we are to grow up in all *aspects* into Him who is the head, *even* Christ, from whom the whole body, being

fitted and held together by what every joint supplies, according to the proper working of each individual part, causes the growth of the body for the building up of itself in love.

This passage tells us that only as we live in mutual ministry with one another will we grow to maturity and experience the purpose that God has for us.

Conclusion

When our country was being founded, Benjamin Franklin said of the leaders, referring to the danger of revolting against England, "We must all hang together, or assuredly we shall all hang separately." And so it is. There is strength in unity. So it is in the church. If we try to make it alone, we "hang" separately. But if we "hang together," we can make it.

Harold Kushner, in his book *When All You Ever Wanted Isn't Enough,*" wrote:

> I was sitting on a beach one summer day, watching two children, a boy and a girl, playing in the sand. They were hard at work building an elaborate sand-castle by the water's edge, with gates and towers and moats and internal passages. Just when they had nearly finished their project, a big wave came along and knocked it down, reducing it to a heap of wet sand. I expected the children to burst into tears, devastated by what had happened to all their hard work. But they surprised me. Instead, they ran up the shore away from the water, laughing and holding hands, and sat down to build another castle. I realized that they had taught me an important lesson. All the things in our lives, all the complicated structures we spend so much time and energy creating are built on sand. Only our relationships with other people endure. Sooner or later, the wave will come along and knock down what we have worked so hard to build up. When that happens, only the person who has somebody's hand to hold will be able to laugh.[6]

The church provides people who will hold our hand when the waves of life destroy the sand castles of life.

In a culture that creates alienation, the church can provide belonging. In a culture that encourages competition, the church can provide cooperation. In a culture that fosters individualism, the church can provide a team. In a culture that encourages self-indulgence, the church can provide something larger than self to live for. The church can provide the ceremonies that draw us together for mutual strength and encouragement during the major experiences of life: births, marriages, crises, victories, and funerals. Belonging to a caring community that is linked to God gives us people to share both our joys and sorrows. In doing so, our joys are doubled and our sorrows are halved.

The Christian life was never meant to be lived alone. Therefore, the second mark of a complete Christian is that he worships God corporately and integrates his entire life with other Christians.

Review for Memory

1. Humans are s _ocial_ b _eings_ because God is a social being, and we are created in His i _mage_. (Page 46)

2. Christians gather for two reasons:
   a. To call p _ublic_ a _ttention_ to the greatness of who God is and what He has done.
   b. To encourage one another to l _ove_ and g _ood_ d _eeds_. (Page 48)

3. Christians are to live their entire lives in r _elationships_ and h _armony_ with other Christians. (Page 51)

4. The Christian life was never meant to be lived a _lone_. (Page 53)

Review for Understanding

Summarize in one paragraph what you think the most important message of this chapter is:

It is not normal or healthy to try to live life alone. God created us to be a body. It is part of imaging Him.

Review for Application

Write out how you think that knowing the information in this chapter will change your behavior toward corporate worship:

It doesn't change so much as renew and reinforce what I already believed

Central Passage: *"And you will know the truth, and the truth will make you free" (John 8:32).*

Mark No. 3: A Complete Christian Grows in Biblical Knowledge

Knowledge is not everything, but everything rests on knowledge. Therefore, the complete Christian masters the Bible so well that the Bible masters him.

Charles Steinmetz was a very bright engineer who worked for General Electric in the first half of the twentieth century. He designed enormous electrical engines that powered entire factories helping further the industrial revolution in the United States. He became a giant in the field of industrial electronics.

After he retired, he reportedly got a call from a vast General Electric factory. Their electric motors had malfunctioned, and none of their technicians knew how to fix them. They asked him to come help them find the problem. Steinmetz walked around the factory testing various parts of the machine complex. After a short time, he took a piece of chalk out of his pocket and put a large X on a particular part of one machine and then left. GE's technicians took the machine apart and discovered that the problem lay immediately behind the X.

Some days later, GE received a bill from Steinmetz for $10,000. This was a hundred years ago, and $10,000 was a vast sum of money. GE executives balked at the huge figure and asked Steinmetz for an itemization of the charge. Steinmetz reportedly sent back an itemization:

Placing one chalk mark:	$	1.00
Knowing where to place it:	$	9,999.00
Total		$10,000.00

Knowledge is power. To gain knowledge is to accumulate the building blocks for whatever your imagination wants to construct. It lays the foundation for everything else that needs to happen. It is knowledge of the truth that sets us free. This is true in all areas of life and especially true of Scripture. A knowledge of Scripture will keep us from mistakes, guide us toward wisdom, strengthen us for the demands of life, empower us for personal achievement, strengthen us against sin, and deepen our relationship with God.

Knowledge Is Not Everything, but Everything Rests on Knowledge

Ignorance is not bliss. Many people have heart-rending tales of woe that could have been avoided if they had known one passage of Scripture. The Bible has unblushing promises of reward and blessing for those who know Scripture well and follow it. In the Christian life, knowledge is not everything, but everything rests on knowledge. So, one of the great challenges of the Christian life is to master the Bible so well that the Bible masters you.

Jesus said in John 8:31–32, "If you continue in My word, *then* you are truly disciples of Mine; and you will know the truth, and the truth will make you free." This tells us that to the degree that we do not know the truth, we will be vulnerable to ignorance and deception.

▶ "A wise man is strong, and a man of knowledge increases power" (Prov. 24:5).

▶ "Take my instruction and not silver, and knowledge rather than choicest gold" (8:10).

▶ "The mind of the intelligent seeks knowledge" (15:14).

▶ "It is not good for a person to be without knowledge" (19:2).

▶ "Grow in the grace and knowledge of our Lord and Savior Jesus Christ" (2 Peter 3:18).

In the spirit of these passages, John Stott, the venerable English pastor, once wrote,

> Knowledge is indispensible to Christian life and service. If we do not use the mind that God has given us, we condemn ourselves to spiritual superficiality and cut ourselves off from many of the riches of God's grace . . . Knowledge is given us to be used, to lead us to higher worship, greater faith, deeper holiness, better service.[1]

Whether we go to Scripture, experience, or common sense, we see that knowledge is a good thing, a powerful thing, and something that a Christian must commit himself to acquiring.

There Are Three Kinds of General Biblical Knowledge

When someone wants to know the Bible, there are three categories of knowledge that he must master.

1. **The facts of the Bible:** the people, places, and events, and some understanding of their chronological order and where they are found in the Bible. Until a person learns his way around in the Bible, he will not be successful in feeding himself from the Scripture. And, until he gains some mastery of the facts of the Bible, he will not be able to find his way around.

2. The doctrines of the Bible: what does the Bible say about God, Christ, and the Holy Spirit? What does the Bible say about angels and demons, salvation, the church, and future things?

3. The principles of Christian living: What does the Bible say about how to live the Christian life, how to pray, and how to know God's will?

The pursuit of knowledge is a matter of the heart, not merely of the head—though it involves the head. It is just that the head must always be connected to the heart. The Holy Spirit must illumine truth for us. Listen to what 1 Corinthians 2:12–13 says:

> Now we have received, not the spirit of the world, but the Spirit who is from God, so that we may know the things freely given to us by God, which things we also speak, not in words taught by human wisdom, but in those taught by the Spirit, combining spiritual *thoughts* with spiritual *words*.

Our capacity to understand spiritual things must grow, just as a baby must grow physically (1 Peter 2:2). A baby cannot will itself to suddenly be six feet tall, and we cannot become suddenly spiritually mature. What we learn today depends on what we learned yesterday. If we did not learn anything yesterday, it inhibits our learning today. There are things God wants to teach us that will satisfy our longing for relationship with Him, smooth out our relationships with others, and give us wisdom for the difficult decisions in life. But we cannot receive it today if we were not diligent students yesterday. The content of the head and the condition of the heart must work together.

There Are Fours Steps to Mastering Biblical Knowledge

There are four distinct steps to gaining deep biblical knowledge: reading, studying, memorizing, and meditating.

1. Reading the Bible: Scripture says in 1 Timothy 4:13, "Give attention to the *public* reading *of Scripture*." The Scriptures were read publicly back then because printing presses did not yet exist, and the average person did not have a copy of the Scriptures. Acts 15:21 suggests that the Scriptures were read each Sabbath in the synagogues and possibly, as a result, also in the early churches. We, however, have the Scriptures readily available to read each day. In order to gain a breadth of biblical knowledge, we can practice the lifelong habit of reading the Bible.

Daily reading of Scripture has a powerful cumulative effect, similar to exercise. Any given day might not seem to make much difference, but combined day after day, month after month, year after year, it can be life changing. Something as simple as reading the Bible five minutes a day can make a powerful contribution to one's Christian life over time. Five minutes a day for 365 days in a year is over thirty hours of Bible reading in a year! Do that for five years, and it is 150 hours. Ten years yields 300 hours of Bible reading!

While any given day might not seem to be life changing, the lifelong practice of reading the Bible each day is. It allows us to maintain a breadth of knowledge of the Bible that we could not maintain any other way.

2. Studying the Bible: In addition to reading the Bible for breadth of knowledge, we must study the Bible for depth of knowledge. Second Timothy 2:15 says, "Be diligent to present yourself approved to God as a workman who does not need to be ashamed, accurately handling the word of truth." To do this, we must do two things.

First, we must put ourselves under good Bible teaching. No one is capable of learning what he could/should from the Bible without the benefit of good teachers. There are several possible categories of Bible teachers.

▶ **Live Teachers**. At least in the early days of your Christian life, you must put yourself under a good live Bible teacher—that is, someone in your church or your town under whom you study the

Bible directly. That way, you can ask questions and learn things that you cannot learn any other way.

▶ **Media Teachers.** Next, you can put yourself under good Bible teachers from media sources including DVDs, the radio, television, or perhaps a correspondence course.

▶ **Books.** Finally, books and written study material can be helpful in deepening your biblical knowledge. These resources can be found in any good Christian bookstore or, increasingly, online.

Second, we must learn how to study the Bible for ourselves. Just as a baby will never grow to physical adulthood unless he stops being spoon-fed and begins to eat for himself, so a spiritual baby will never grow to spiritual adulthood until he begins to feed himself spiritually from the Bible. There are good books and Internet resources on how to study the Bible, but, for many people, this capacity is developed as they study under good teachers. This requires, however, that you not just show up for each lesson and do nothing in between. It requires that you study for yourself between lessons.

3. Memorizing the Bible: In Psalm 119:148 we read, "My eyes anticipate the night watches, that I may meditate on Your word." A person cannot meditate on the Word in the middle of the night unless he has the Word memorized. You read and study the Bible so you can master the Word. You memorize and meditate on the Bible so that the Word will master you. It is not uncommon for people to know the Bible well but not be mastered by it in their thoughts, emotions, and actions. Memorization and meditation on Scripture completes that transition.

Many people do not memorize passages thoroughly enough. Like students cramming for an exam, they memorize just well enough to squeak by and then go on to others. However, it is vital to memorize verses so thoroughly that someone can shake you awake in the middle of the night and say, "Quick, what is Romans 12:1–2?" and you could rattle it off without delay.

4. Meditating on the Bible: In verses we have already seen, the Scripture says, "How blessed is the man . . . [whose] delight is in the law of the LORD, and in His law he meditates day and night. He will be like a tree *firmly* planted by streams of water, which yields its fruit in its season . . . and in whatever he does, he prospers" (Psalm 1: 1–3). Add to that Joshua 1:8, "This book of the law shall not depart from your mouth, but you shall meditate on it day and night, so that you may be careful to do according to all that is written in it; for then you will make your way prosperous, and then you will have success."

> When we meditate on Scripture, the Holy Spirit will open the meaning of Scripture up to us on a level not possible any other way. First Corinthians 2:12–13 says, "Now we have received, not the spirit of the world, but the Spirit who is from God, so that we may know the things freely given to us by God, which things we also speak, not in words taught by human wisdom, but in those taught by the Spirit."

> When we meditate on Scripture, the Holy Spirit will open the meaning of Scripture up to us on a level not possible any other way.

Meditation on Scripture involves <u>mentally rehearsing Scripture</u> passages, allowing them to go over and over in our minds as we ponder the potential implications of the truth for our lives. As we think of something again and again, we gain insight into the Scripture that does not come to us with a lesser degree of mental focus. We take each sentence, sometimes each word, and ponder its meaning. Some days we may not receive new insight. Other days we may. But regardless of whether or not we receive any new insights, the process of thinking about a passage over and over again, day after day, drives the truth of the Scripture more deeply into our hearts and minds and gives the Holy Spirit opportunities to enlighten us more fully. This creates a deeper knowledge, deeper understanding, and deeper acceptance of the truth than we experience any other way.

There Are Five Promises for Mastering the Bible

1. **Power to change:** As we master Scripture, we can experience spiritual growth and change. (1 Tim. 1:5)

2. **Power for ministry:** As we master Scripture we are equipped for every good work. (2 Tim. 3:16–17)

3. **Power over sin:** When we hide His word in our hearts, we will not sin against Him. (Ps. 119:9, 11)

4. **Power in spiritual warfare:** Every time Jesus rebuffed the temptations of the devil, He did so by quoting Scripture. (Matt. 4:1–11)

5. **Spiritual success:** As we meditate on Scripture, we are lifted to spiritual success in what we do. (Ps. 1:1–3)

Conclusion

Knowledge is power, and it is one of our greatest weapons. I read some time back of a research scientist who occasionally logged onto the Internet and played simulated war games with other people after a long, hard day at the laboratory. One night, he was teamed up with an apparent military genius, whose knowledge of tactics, grasp of strategy, and anticipation of the opponent's moves were uncanny. He and his partner won six wars against their Internet foes in one evening. He was astonished when, after the last game, his partner said that his mom had just told him he had to go to bed. "Go to bed?! How old are you?" the research scientist typed. His genius partner typed back, "Twelve. How old are you?" After only a slight hesitation, the scientist responded, "Eight."

Yes, knowledge is power. It can put a twelve-year-old on a par with adults, can raise a person of humble beginnings to a position of influence, and can provide answers for many of life's problems. All else being equal, knowledge can make the difference between a successful life and a life of frustration and defeat.

Therefore, the third mark of complete Christians is that he or she learns what is necessary, mastering the Bible so well that the Bible masters him or her.

Review for Memory

1. Knowledge is not everything, but everything r _exts_ on knowledge. (Page 56)

2. There are three kinds of biblical knowledge:
    a. F _acts_ of the Bible
    b. D _octrines_ of the Bible
    c. P _rinciples_ of Christian living. (Page 57–58)

3. There are four steps to mastering biblical knowledge:
    a. R _eading_ the Bible
    b. S _tudying_ the Bible
    c. M _emorizing_ the Bible
    d. M _editating_ on the Bible (Page 59–61)

4. There are five promises for mastering the Bible:
    a. Power to c _hange_
    b. Power for m _inistry_
    c. Power over s _in_
    d. Power in spiritual w _arfare_
    e. Spiritual s _uccess_ (Page 62)

Review for Understanding

Summarize in one paragraph what you think the most important message of this chapter is:

The importance of deeply knowing Scripture cannot be over-emphasized. The more we interact with it, the more it will change us.

Review for Application

Write out how you think that knowing this will change your behavior toward gaining a strong understanding of Scripture:

I just really need the memorization and meditation steps.

CHAPTER 7

Central Passage: "*You shall be holy, for I am holy*" (1 Peter 1:16).

Mark No. 4: A Complete Christian Grows in a Christlike Lifestyle

A Christian is measured not primarily by what he knows or what he does, but by who he is. Therefore, a complete Christian commits to being conformed to the character image of Christ.

People are not always what they seem. For example, Frank Abagnale, Jr., is one of the most famous impostors in American history. In his early life, he assumed identities as a Pan-American World Airways pilot, a Georgian medical doctor, a US Bureau of Prisons agent, and a lawyer. A man of extraordinary intelligence and uncanny perception, he was not only able to convince people of these identities but also to perform the essential functions of each! His primary crime was check fraud. He escaped from police custody twice—once from a taxiing airliner and once from prison. After serving fewer than five years in prison, he went straight and began work with the FBI as a consultant and lecturer and established Abagnale and

Associates, a financial fraud consultancy, primarily helping banks avoid fraud against them. A movie entitled *Catch Me If You Can*, starring Leonardo DiCaprio as Abagnale and Tom Hanks as an FBI agent always after him, was based on his life.

As a world-class imposter, it is amazing how different Abagnale really was from what he seemed. It seemed that he was an airline pilot. But he was not. It seemed he was a doctor. But he was not. It seemed he was a lawyer. But he was not. Something is terribly out of sync when someone appears to be one thing, but is really another.

Each of us as Christians has a great challenge to live like who we really are. We are children of God, we are born again, we have the Holy Spirit living within us, we have the Bible to guide us, and we have the challenge to reach the world for Christ. There is something terribly wrong if the people who look at us see an impostor and not the person we really are. **Our great challenge is to live consistently with who we are in Christ.**

In an example that is perhaps more striking for Christians, Chuck Colson tells the story in his book, *Loving God*, of Mickey Cohen, a mobster and number-one bad boy in Los Angeles, involved in illegal gambling.

Mickey was rich and powerful, and though loyal to his friends, he was ruthless with anyone who crossed him or failed him. The bottom fell out of his life when the IRS caught up with him, and he spent time in prison. One night, after spending time with Billy Graham, Cohen supposedly became a Christian. Yet, he did not distance himself from his criminal past.

Finally, a friend confronted him, telling him that as a new Christian, he ought to be putting as much distance as possible between himself and his old mob connections.

There is something terribly wrong if the people who look at us see an impostor and not the person we really are.

Mickey replied, "You never told me that I had to give up my career. You never told me I had to give up my old friends. There are Christian movie stars, Christian athletes, Christian businessmen. So what's wrong with a Christian gangster! If I have to give up all that, count me out!!!"[1]

Cohen saw no connection between his faith and his lifestyle. Yet the Bible says, "So this I say, and affirm together with the Lord, that you walk no longer just as the [non-Christians] also walk, in the futility of their mind, being darkened in their understanding, excluded from the life of God" (Eph. 4:17–18). There is to be a difference between how Christians and non-Christians live.

Today, the disconnect between what many claim to believe and how they actually live is getting wider and wider as our culture drifts further and further away from biblical truth. It is not unheard of for celebrities of our day—movie stars, rock stars, professional athletes— to claim Christianity and wear crosses around their necks while living an openly immoral lifestyle. This, then, makes it more difficult to perceive the difference between a Christian and a non-Christian, especially for children and newer believers.

Christians are not supposed to live as non-Christians. We are supposed to live in righteousness and holiness. We are supposed to be changed when we give our lives to Jesus. We do not have the freedom to simply conform to the world around us. We are called to rise to a higher world.

We started out by saying that a Christian is measured not primarily by what he knows or what he does, but by who he is. It is important what you know. Jesus said, "You will know the truth, and the truth will make you free" (John 8:32). So we must know something, and it is important what we know. It is also important what we do. James wrote that "faith without works is dead" (James 2:26). But to know the truth and to be active in ministry without having Christlike character is hypocrisy. If we are to take our faith seriously, we must understand that it is a whole faith, not a compartmentalized faith. What we know and what we do must be supported by who we are.

Concerning our character, the Bible has some impressive lists of things we are supposed to not be.

Galatians 5:18–21 says that we are not to display "immorality, impurity, sensuality, idolatry, sorcery, enmities, strife, jealousy, outbursts of anger, disputes, dissensions, factions, envying, drunkenness, carousing, and things like these."

Ephesians 5:3–5 says that we are not to display immorality, impurity, greed, filthiness, silly talk, and coarse jesting.

Colossians 3:5–9 says that we are not to display immorality, impurity, passion, evil desire, greed, anger, wrath, malice, slander, abusive speech, and lies.

This is by no means a complete list, but it is a strong list of activities that the Bible says call down the displeasure of God on those who do them (Eph. 5:6, Col. 3:6). Apparently, in terms of consequences, some sins are worse than others, and these are some of the bad ones.

Juxtaposed against that impressive list of things that we are not supposed to be is an equally impressive list of things we are supposed to be.

Galatians 5:22–23 says that we are supposed to display love, joy, peace, patience, kindness, goodness, faithfulness, gentleness, and self-control.

1 Timothy 3:2–5 says that we are supposed to be above reproach, temperate, prudent, respectable, hospitable, able to teach, not addicted to wine or pugnacious, but gentle, peaceable, and free from the love of money.

1 Corinthians 13:4–5 says that we are to be patient, kind, not envious, not proud, not arrogant, not act unbecomingly, not seek our own, not provoked, and not take into account a wrong suffered.

In 1 Corinthians 11:1, Paul says, "Be imitators of me, just as I also am of Christ." In calling us to these character traits, Paul is calling us to imitate his character, which is also the character of Jesus. **So, Scripture teaches that Jesus is the standard for Christian character. We are created in His image, and He calls us to emulate His character.** It is a very big job. It is a bigger job than merely knowing what we need to know or doing what we need to do.

Romans 8:29 tells us that "those whom He foreknew, He also predestined *to become* conformed to the image of His Son." First John 3:2 tells us, "Beloved, now we are children of God, and it has not appeared as yet what we will be. We know that when He appears, we will be like Him, because we will see Him just as He is." It is God's intention that we become like Jesus in our character and lifestyle.

> The gap is a wide one between who we are and who [Christ] is.

However, knowing that we should be like Christ and actually being like Him are two different things. We may even desperately want to be like Him and still fall short. There are two reasons for this. One is that Jesus is so far beyond us that we will never be completely like Him. The gap is a wide one between who we are and who He is. Another reason is that becoming like Him is a process. That is, we may desire to be like Him, but even then, we must grow into His likeness.

In 1 Peter 2:2, we read, "Like newborn babies, long for the pure milk of the word, so that by it you may grow in respect to salvation." This makes it clear that once we become Christians, we must grow into Christlikeness. This, of course, takes time. It also takes guided effort. Without guided effort, we merely become older Christians. With guided effort, we become more mature Christians.

Five Parts to the Spiritual Growth Process

There are five essential parts to our guided-growth process. They include:

1. The Word of God

2. The Work of God

3. Personal Commitment

4. Other Believers

5. Time and Trials

If we give adequate attention to each of these five areas, we can become spiritually mature with our character matching who we have become in Christ. If we leave any of the five out, or do not give adequate attention to any of them, we will not become mature in Christ.

The Word of God

We have already seen that the Word of God is required for spiritual maturity. The testimony of Scripture to this fact is powerful.

▶ "The word of God is living and active and sharper than any two-edged sword" (Heb. 4:12).

▶ "You will know the truth, and the truth will make you free" (John 8:32).

▶ "Your word is truth" (John 17:17).

▶ "All Scripture is inspired by God and profitable for teaching, for reproof, for correction, for training in righteousness; so that the man of God may be adequate, equipped for every good work" (2 Tim. 3:16–17).

▶ "This book of the law shall not depart from your mouth, but you shall meditate on it day and night, so that you may be careful to do according to all that is written in it; for then you will make your way prosperous, and then you will have success" (Josh. 1:8).

The Word of God gives us the truth, the wisdom, and the power to grow spiritually. Without the Scriptures, we cannot grow to maturity in Christ.

The Work of God

To grow spiritually, we need the work of God. Scripture tell us that:

▶ Unless the Holy Spirit illumines our mind, we cannot understand the deeper things of the Scripture (1 Cor. 2:10–12).

▶ The fruit of the Spirit is the fruit of the Spirit, not the fruit of self-effort (Gal. 5:22–23).

▶ "Work out your salvation with fear and trembling; for it is God who is at work in you, both to will and to work for *His* good pleasure" (Phil. 2:12–13).

This passage is not teaching that we must do good works in order to earn our salvation. That misimpression is put to rest in Ephesians 2:8–9, which makes clear that our salvation is a gift of God, not a result of our good works. Rather, it is saying that once we have salvation, we must express it and live it out consistently because it is God who is working in our hearts to do just that. God works in us first, then we respond.

The work of God gives us the impetus and the power to grow spiritually. Without the work of God, we cannot grow to spiritual maturity.

Personal Commitment

To grow to spiritual maturity, we need personal commitment, which is the other side of the work of God.

▶ We must respond to God's promptings in our life "to will and work for *His* good pleasure," as we read in Philippians 2:12–13, to enter fully into God's spiritual growth process.

▶ Romans 12:1 urges us to present our bodies as a living sacrifice to God. A living sacrifice means, of course, complete commitment.

▶ First Corinthians 9:25–27 says, "Everyone who competes in the games exercises self-control in all things. They then *do it* to receive a perishable wreath, but we an imperishable. Therefore . . . I discipline my body and make it my slave, so that, after I have preached to others, I myself will not be disqualified."

God has ordained that there are some things He must do and some things we must do for us to grow spiritually. God does the work of God, and man does the work of man. Man cannot do the work of God, and God will not do the work of man. Without personal commitment, we cannot grow to maturity in Christ.

Other Believers

To grow to maturity, we need other believers. As we saw in chapter 5, God never intended for us to be able to live the Christian life alone. It has been said that the Christian life is more easily caught than taught. That is why, in Scripture, the Christian life is nurtured in the context of relationships.

▶ Romans 12:4–5 says, "Just as we have many members in one body and all the members do not have the same function, so we, who are many, are one body in Christ, and individually members of one another."

▶ Ephesians 4:15–16 says, "The whole body [is] fitted and held together by what every joint supplies, according to the proper working of each individual part, [and that is what] causes the growth of the body for the building up of itself in love."

Therefore, one thing we can do to encourage our own spiritual growth is to spend time with other Christians and integrate our entire lives with other believers. There are a number of levels on which we spend time with other Christians. God has ordained that we cannot make it alone. Without other believers, we cannot grow to maturity in Christ.

Time and Trials

To grow to spiritual maturity requires time and trials. Spiritual growth takes time, just as physical growth takes time. As we saw, 1 Peter 2:2 says, "Like newborn babies, long for the pure milk of the word, so that by it you may grow in respect to salvation." While time is passing as we are growing, we will encounter trials, and these trials are essential to our spiritual maturity. From examples we see in various places in Scripture, these trials might be health problems, financial challenges, persecution for one's faith, circumstances falling apart, and so on. James 1:2–4 says, "Consider it all joy, my brethren, when you encounter various trials, knowing that the testing of your faith produces endurance. And let endurance have *its* perfect result, so that you may be perfect and complete, lacking in nothing." If we understand and cooperate with this spiritual growth process, we will grow as rapidly as the will of God allows.

We cannot be holy in a hurry, and the road to transformation always goes through the tunnel of trials. Without time and trials, we cannot grow to maturity in Christ.

Conclusion

As we give ourselves to the spiritual growth process that God has ordained, we grow spiritually, being transformed from who we once were into who Christ is. In doing so, our lifestyles become consistent with who we became in Christ when we came to faith in Him. We begin to experience the fullness of life that God intends us to have.

C. S. Lewis shed light on this when he wrote:

> When a man turns to Christ and seems to be getting on pretty well (in the sense that some of his bad habits are corrected), he often feels that it would now be natural if things went fairly smoothly. When troubles come along—illnesses, money troubles, new kinds of temptation—he is disappointed. These things, he feels, might have been necessary to rouse him and make him repent in his bad old days; but why now? Because God is forcing him on, or up, to a higher level: putting him into situations where he will have to be very much braver, or more patient, or more loving, than he ever dreamed of being before. It seems to us all unnecessary: but that is because we have not yet had the slightest notion of the tremendous thing he means to make of us.
>
> Imagine yourself a living house. God comes in to rebuild that house. At first, perhaps you can understand what he is doing. He is getting the drains right and stopping the leaks in the roof and so on: you knew that those jobs needed doing so you are not surprised. But presently he starts knocking the house about in a way that hurts abominably and does not seem to make sense. What on earth is he up to? The explanation is that he is building quite a different house from the one you thought of—throwing out a new wing here, putting on an extra floor there, running up towers, making courtyards. You thought you were going to be made into a decent little cottage: but he is building a palace.
>
> If we let him—for we can prevent him, if we choose—he will make the feeblest and filthiest of us into a . . . dazzling, radiant,

immortal creature, pulsating all through with such energy and joy and wisdom and love as we cannot now imagine, a bright, stainless mirror which reflects back to God perfectly (though, of course, on a smaller scale) his own boundless power and delight and goodness.[2]

Yes . . . transformation is our destiny . . . it is God's desire for us . . . yes even His serious intention—something He will do, if we will but trust Him and obey Him. The price is everything we have, and in return, God promises to give us everything we long for.

Our lifestyle is at the heart of our Christian experience. It is not enough to know. It is not enough to do. We must be. All that we know and all that we do only takes on credibility as it rests on the foundation of a Christlike character and a biblical lifestyle.

So, a Christian is measured not primarily by what he knows or what he does but by who he is. Therefore, a complete Christian commits to being conformed to the character image of Christ.

Review for Memory

1. Our great challenge, as Christians, is to live c onsistently, with who we are in Christ. (Page 66)

2. Scripture makes it very clear that J esus is the standard for Christian character. (Page 69)

3. There are five parts to the spiritual growth process:
   a. The W ord of God
   b. The W ork of God
   c. Personal C ommitment
   d. Other B elievers
   e. Time and T rials (Page 70)

Review for Understanding

Summarize in one paragraph what you think the most important message of this chapter is:

Jesus is our example for growth.

Review for Application

Write out how you think that knowing this will influence your Christian lifestyle:

_____

_____

_____

_____

_____

_____

_____

_____

_____

_____

CHAPTER 8

Central Passage: "As each one has received a special gift, employ it in serving one another" (1 Peter 4:10).

Mark No. 5: A Complete Christian Grows in Ministry Skills

God gives each person a job to do and gifts to do it with. Therefore, a complete Christian discovers and uses his spiritual gifts and shares his faith with others.

I once read the story of a duck that hatched under the watchful eye of a motherly collie dog. Because ducks imprint on the first thing they see when they are hatched, the duck thought it was a dog. It followed the collie on its daily rounds around the farm, slept with the dog under the front porch in the heat of the day, and when a car drove into the driveway, it exploded from under the porch with the barking dog, quacking and flapping furiously while trying to peck the tires.

However, in spite of the fact that the duck took on many mannerisms of the dog, it proved time and time again that it was a duck. It quacked instead of barked. It rose up on tiptoes and flapped its wings after sitting for long periods of time. And, whenever it saw water, it immediately chugged into it and started swimming around. These were all things the collie never did.

The point is, there are some things that are simply in us. We do them because we were created to do them. We are hardwired by God for certain things. For example, when we take personality inventories, such as Myers-Briggs or DiSC, they consistently reveal our inherent God-wiring for life and ministry. They reveal that we are natural leaders or list-makers, introverted or extroverted. We will act consistently with that God-wiring in the circumstances of life; and if we get into a situation that demands that we act contrary to our God-wiring, it can create significant stress for us.

. . . if we get into a situation that demands that we act contrary to our God-wiring, it can create significant stress for us.

That fact is made even more important in the lives of Christians when paired with the fact that God has created us for good works. Ephesians 2:10 says, "For we are His workmanship, created in Christ Jesus for good works, which God prepared beforehand so that we would walk in them." This verse is telling us that before we were ever born, God created good works that He wants us to do.

If that is the case, then the good works that we are created to do will mesh with how we are God-wired. When we mesh how we are God-wired for ministry with the ministries that require our unique God-wiring, we find ourselves in the sweet spot of life in which we are deeply satisfied and wonderfully effective.

This fact is exemplified by the unique characteristics of dogs. On one hand, bird dogs love to hunt birds. Take them to an open field by the edge of a woods, the bird dogs will zigzag back and forth by the hour, nose to the ground, hunting for pheasant or quail. They are never happier.

On the other hand, sled dogs love to run. Put them in a harness in front of a snow sled with a dozen other dogs in below-zero temperature in a frozen wasteland, and they will happily run for seventy-five miles a day, their doggy faces split in half by wide, silly grins.

But what if you were to switch the dogs? What if you were to put a sled dog in a bean field and the bird dog in a sled harness? The two would be miserable. Out of place. Frustrated. Defeated. The bird dog would be freezing and wondering why it is being tied down to that metal monstrosity. The sled dog would be wondering where all the snow is, where the other dogs are, and why they are running back and forth in one field rather than taking off cross country.

Like those dogs, we are each created by God with certain inner hardwiring in our temperament and personality. In addition, we have all been give spiritual gifts—an added dimension of uniqueness that each person possesses—which help guide us into what ministries God has prepared for us.

We each have been given a job to do and specific God-wiring and gifts with which to do it, and we will never be wholly fulfilled until we are doing what we were created by God to do.

Christians Are Given Spiritual Gifts

While temperaments and personalities are determined by observation, the Bible actually speaks of spiritual gifts. The apostle Peter, in 1 Peter 4:10, wrote, "As each one has received a *special* gift, employ it in serving one another as good stewards of the manifold grace of God."

In Romans 12:4–6, the apostle Paul builds the case for spiritual gifts, writing, "For just as we have many members in one body and all the members do not have the same function, so we, who are many, are one body in Christ, and individually members of one another. Since we have gifts that differ according to the grace given to us, *each of us is to exercise them accordingly.*"

These passages make two things clear. We have each been given spiritual gifts, and God expects us to use them. By calling us to use our spiritual gifts in service to others, God is setting us up for a life of deep meaning and purpose. **Because we were created by Him for**

good works, we will only experience full satisfaction in life as we are using our gifts to do the works He has prepared for us.

There are three different kinds of gifts referred to in the New Testament:

1. There are office gifts given to those who serve the church at large including apostle, prophet, evangelist, and pastor-teacher (Eph. 4:11–12).

2. There are special gifts that appear to be given not only for a specific purpose/need of the moment but also for validating the message of Christianity to those who have never heard or believed (1 Cor. 12:7–11).

3. There are service gifts, which are non-miraculous gifts that correspond to ministries that all of us should do, but some individuals are gifted for greater impact in those ministries (Rom. 12:6–8). In this chapter, we are referring only to the service gifts.

The Bible does not tell us how to learn what our spiritual gifts are or even that we should learn them. It just tells us to get busy being faithful at all the things that are in the service gifts list in Romans 12:6–8. For example, below is a chart that lists the service-oriented spiritual gifts on the left. To the right is a biblical command that tells us all that we are all responsible to do the activity of the spiritual gift. The significance is that we are all to help, but some have the gift of helps. We are all to give, but some have the gift of giving. So we are all to be responsible to these activities, but some of us will be gifted for greater impact than others. This is adapted from my book *What You Need to Know About the Holy Spirit*:

. . . we will only experience full satisfaction in life as we are using our gifts to do the works He has prepared for us.

Spiritual Gift	Command to All
Helping:	"In everything I showed you that by working hard in this manner you must help the weak." (Acts 20:35)
Teaching:	"Go therefore . . . teaching them to observe all that I commanded you." (Matt. 28:19–20)
Exhortation:	"Not forsaking our own assembling together . . . but encouraging *one another*." (Heb. 10:25)
Giving:	"Each one *must do* just as he has purposed in his heart, not grudgingly or under compulsion, for God loves a cheerful giver." (2 Cor. 9:7)
Leading:	"You also became imitators of us and of the Lord, having received the word in much tribulation with the joy of the Holy Spirit, so that you became an example to all the believers in Macedonia and in Achaia." (1 Thess. 1:6–7)
Mercy:	"Blessed are the merciful, for they shall receive mercy." (Matt. 5:7)[1]

It is possible to take spiritual gift inventories now that help us identify what our spiritual gift(s) might be, and they can be helpful. However, the key is to become active in service to others, and as we do, we will discover that we enjoy some things more than others, are drawn to them, and are more effective at them. It is through being active in ministry that we most effectively learn our spiritual gifts.

It is as we become active in living a life outside ourselves, higher than ourselves, and greater than ourselves that we begin to taste the fullness of joy that is offered to us.

Harold Kushner makes this observation in his book *When All You Ever Wanted Isn't Enough*:

> Our souls are not hungry for fame, comfort, wealth, or power. Those rewards create almost as many problems as they solve. Our souls are hungry for meaning, for the sense that we have figured out how to live so that our lives matter, so that the world will be at least a little bit different for our having passed through it. Happiness does

not come by pursuing happiness. You become happy by living a life that means something. The happiest people you know are probably not the richest or most famous, probably not the ones who are working hardest at being happy by reading articles and buying the books and latching on to the latest fads. I suspect that the happiest people you know are the ones who work at being kind, helpful, and reliable, and happiness sneaks into their lives while they are busy doing those things. You don't become happy by pursuing happiness. It is always a by-product, never a primary goal.[2]

Christians are never fully satisfied until they are using their spiritual gifts in service to God and sharing their faith in Christ with others. We need a sense of purpose in life, and we will not have it until we are doing what God has gifted and called us to do.

Someone once said that if George Washington had tried to be an inventor and Benjamin Franklin had tried to be a general, we would all be sitting around in the dark speaking with a British accent. But fortunately, those two men got it right and changed the world. When we get it right with our calling and giftedness, we can help change our part of the world.

Christians Are Called to Share Their Faith in Christ

In addition, part of the good works God has prepared for us to do is to share our faith in Christ with others. In Matthew 28:19–20, we read what is called the Great Commission: "Go therefore and make disciples of all the nations, baptizing them in the name of the Father and the Son and the Holy Spirit, teaching them to observe all that I commanded you."

After Jesus' resurrection, the entire focus of the church was to take the message of the gospel to those who have never heard. In Acts 1:8, Jesus said to His followers, "You shall be My witnesses both in Jerusalem, and in all Judea and Samaria, and even to the remotest part of the earth."

So, in addition to learning how to use our spiritual gifts, God calls everyone to share their faith, and He has gifted each of us to share our faith in a way that is consistent with our God-wiring. **We may not find deep satisfaction in sharing our faith the way someone else shares his faith, but we will find deep satisfaction sharing our faith the way God has created us to share it.**

Of this responsibility, James Packer, in his book *Evangelism and the Sovereignty of God,* has written with compelling and crystal-clear precision the essence of our responsibility:

> Evangelism, we have learned, is a task appointed to all God's people everywhere. It is the task of communicating a message from the Creator to rebel mankind. The message begins with information and ends with an invitation. The information concerns God's work of making His Son a perfect Saviour for sinners. The invitation is God's summons to mankind generally to come to the Saviour and find life. God commands all men everywhere to repent and promises forgiveness and restoration to all who do. The Christian is sent into the world as God's herald and Christ's ambassador, to broadcast this message as widely as he can. This is both his duty (because God commands it and love to our neighbour requires it) and his privilege (because it is a great thing to speak for God and to take our neighbour the remedy—the only remedy—that can save him from the terrors of spiritual death). Our job, then, is to go to our fellow-men and tell them the gospel of Christ and try by every means to make it clear to them; to remove as best we can any difficulties that they may find in it, to impress them with its seriousness, and to urge them to respond to it. This is our abiding responsibility; it is a basic part of our Christian calling.[3]

What could be clearer? And what could be more compelling? Just as we are glad someone shared the gospel with us, so we should share the gospel with others. It is our responsibility and our privilege. But we will typically be more faithful and more fulfilled if we find a way to share our faith that is consistent with how we are gifted by God. Hmm...

For example, if we are deeply introverted, it is not likely that we will be satisfied and effective doing street preaching, using a bullhorn to arrest the attention of hundreds of people passing by on a crowded intersection. Street preachers are typically extremely extroverted with a compulsion to encourage and even challenge people in their lifestyles. An extremely introverted person may find it more effective to develop relationships with others over time and, when the moment is right, give a personal account of one's own salvation experience and gently give the friend an opportunity to respond.

So ask yourself, *how could I become comfortable sharing my faith? What could I see myself doing to spread the gospel? Have I been a Christian for a while? Am I fully engaged in evangelism? Or am I hiding from a life of evangelism because I have not yet found my sweet spot for sharing my faith?* If you put your mind in creative mode and envision the highest and most natural involvement you might have in evangelism, you can begin to enter a life of involvement and satisfaction in evangelism that brings deep purpose and meaning to your life.

I have never heard this take on evangelism styles before

Conclusion

If you could wave a magic wand and do whatever you wanted to do for Christ and knew that you would be successful, what would you do? If you could take your temperament, personality, spiritual gifts, your background and education, your experience, your successes and failures, and use them for their highest good, what might that look like?

When you answer that question, you are on your way to a fuller picture of the possibilities of the good works that God has prepared you to walk in. What He has for you might not look exactly like your magic wand, but as you begin to think that way, the Lord can lead you into the good works He has for you.

God has a job for each of us. He has gifted us to do the job. My job is different than yours, and yours from mine. Our job is to give ourselves to God, and then ask, *Dear Lord, what do You want me to do?* The answers you get will be different from mine, but together, we make up the body of Christ and can be used by Him to extend His kingdom into the lost and needy world around us. Do not fear the process. Abandon your gifts to God. Abandon yourself to God. It is your purpose. It is your meaning. It is your destiny. And it is your joy and satisfaction. It is what you were created to do.

God gives each person a job to do and gifts to do it with. Therefore, the fifth mark of a complete Christian is that he discovers and uses his spiritual gifts and shares his faith with others.

Review for Memory

1. God gives each person a j_*do*__ to do and g_*ift*_____ to do it with. (Page 85)

2. Because we were created by Him for g_*ood*_____ w_*orks*_____, we will only experience full satisfaction in life as we are using our gifts to do the works He has prepared for us. (Pages 79–80)

3. Part of the "good works" God has prepared for us to do is to share our f_*aith*_____ in C_*hrist*_____ with others. (Page 82)

4. We may not find deep satisfaction in sharing our faith the way s_*omeone*_____ else shares his faith, but we will find deep satisfaction sharing our faith the way God has c_*reated*_____ us to share it. (Page 83)

Review for Understanding

Summarize in one paragraph what you think the most important message of this chapter is:

Every person has been uniquely gifted by God to do the good work He has planned for us to do. We discover what these are by getting involved in ministry.

Review for Application

Write out how you think that knowing this will influence your ministry skill development:

I am intrigued by the idea of evangelizing based on my spiritual gifts. I would like to play with this idea & get creative with how I share the gospel.

Central Passage: "From [Him] the whole body, being fitted and held together by what every joint supplies, according to the proper working of each individual part, causes the growth of the body for the building up of itself in love" (Eph. 4:16).

Mark No. 6: A Complete Christian Impacts the Church

Christians are family and should care for one another. Therefore, a complete Christian uses his time, talent, and treasure for the welfare of the church and other Christians.

Some things are more difficult than they first seem. Take the Washington Monument for example. It seems simple enough when you first look at it—a simple marble stick poking high into the Washington, D.C., sky. However, it is ten times as high (555 feet) as it is wide at the base (fifty-five feet). How in the world did they keep it from falling over? What would happen to it in a hurricane? Ever try to stack children's blocks ten times as high as the base? You get some idea of the magnitude of architectural challenges in keeping something that high and that heavy from falling over after a while. The walls are fifteen feet thick at the base and only eighteen inches at the top. It sits on a foundation that is thirty-six-feet deep. It is weighted and scaled and grounded so that it is not in danger of falling over. The architects knew what they were doing when they built it. It will still be standing when all of us are gone.

Or take Mt. Rushmore. If you have ever tried to shape clay figures with your fingers and have them not turn out the way you wanted them to look, you can only imagine how difficult it must have been to blast away at acres of granite with 24,000 pounds of dynamite and have the results look like American presidents.

When you look at the Washington Monument or Mt. Rushmore just as objects, it is easy to take them for granted. But when you ponder the information, planning, and creativity behind them, they are works of engineering genius as well as art.

> [The church] is more difficult than it seems and more important than it seems.

Not only are some things more difficult than they first seem, but also some things are more important than they first seem. For example, wetlands seem to be soggy wastelands good for nothing but breeding mosquitoes. Yet they collect and filter water before it goes underground, neutralize pesticides and other contaminants, provide habitats for a cavalcade of animals, and are generally an essential feature of a healthy ecosystem.

Trade winds seem random and unimportant, yet without them, cold would collect at the poles, heat would collect at the equator, pollution would collect at the site, and rain would fall only in one place—making life on earth as we know it impossible.

Yes, some things are more difficult than they seem and more important than they seem.

The church falls into both categories. It is more difficult than it seems and more important than it seems. Jesus said, "I will build My church; and the gates of Hades will not overpower it" (Matt. 16:18). That tells us how important it is. Then, Scripture after Scripture addressing sin and problems in various early churches tells us how difficult it is (1 Cor. 5; 2 Tim. 2–3; James 3–4).

However, because of how important it is, and in spite of how difficult it is, the complete Christian impacts the church.

Christians Serve the Lord by Serving the Church

Jesus wants us to treat our brothers and sisters in Christ the same way we treat Him, and vice versa. In Matthew 25:40 Jesus teaches that when we serve the least of Christ's brothers, we serve Him. In Acts 9:4, Jesus asks Saul why he is persecuting Him. But Saul was not persecuting Jesus. He had never met Jesus. Saul was persecuting Christians, the church. Jesus considered Saul's persecution of the church to be persecution of Him. So, how we treat the church is how Jesus considers we treat Him. We serve the Lord by serving the church.

Beyond that, the New Testament clearly states that Christians are members of one another (Rom. 12:5). We are all members of one body (Eph. 4:12) and living stones in one temple (1 Peter 2:5), children in one family (1 Tim. 5:1), commanded by God to live "all for one and one for all." We are not just one with Christ, but we are one with each other and should act accordingly.

So, as we read Scripture to see how we should treat the church, we learn that a complete Christian uses his time, talent, and treasure for the welfare of the church and other Christians.

Christians Serve the Church with Their Time and Talents

Someone once asked Sir Winston Churchill if he was a pillar of the church. Churchill responded, "I'm more of a flying buttress: I support it from the outside."

Well, that is probably better than not supporting it at all, but Christians need to support the church from the inside. As part of one's commitment to a body of believers, the Christian should also serve that body with his time and talent. In Galatians 6:10, we see that we are to do good to all men but especially those who are of the household of faith. We also see passages instructing us to do things for one another. Those commands cannot be fulfilled without our giving of our time and talent.

1. Minister to one another with our spiritual gifts. Romans 12:6 says we are to exercise our gifts for the benefit of other Christians. This includes the gifts of faith, service, exhortation, teaching, giving, and mercy.

2. Do good to one another. Galatians 6:10 says while we have time, let us do good to all men, but especially those who are of the household of faith.

3. Help disadvantaged in the church. James 1:27 says that we are to visit orphans and widows in their distress.

4. Help poor Christians. Galatians 2:10 says that we are to remember the poor Christians among us.

5. Encourage other Christians. First Thessalonians 5:11 says we are to encourage and build up one another.

This is not a technical list giving us the freedom to ignore whatever is not on the list. Rather, it is a description of a spirit that should be true of the church. All too often, members of the church do not see themselves as one with the other members. All too often, we treat members of the church the same way the world treats others, and this diminishes the pleasure of belonging to the church as well as diminishing the effectiveness of the church.

Harold Kushner once wrote:

> Some people have to be very competitive to reach the top, and once they have gotten there, they find it hard to break the habit of competitiveness. They are not able to relax and chat with me. They feel

that they have to impress me by telling me how successful they are, by dropping the names of important people they know. Sometimes they start an intellectual argument with me, trying to show me that they know more about my subject than I do. On those occasions, I find myself wondering why they feel they have to be so competitive, why they have to respond to a guest in their home as a competitor to be challenged, and whether part of the price they have paid for their success, part of their bargain with the devil, if you will, is that they keep transforming friends into enemies.[1]

It is a terrible temptation to view people as competitors when we should be ministering to them or simply fellowshipping with them. We are supposed to love people and use things, but our temptation is to turn it around—to love things and use people. Scripture tells us not to do that. You are part of one another. You are terribly important to God, and you are terribly important to one another. Live like that! Serve one another.

Christians Serve the Church with Their Treasure

We worship God when we give Him our treasure with a willing heart. In Matthew 2:11, we see the wise men coming to worship Jesus. When they saw Him, they "fell to the ground and worshiped Him." Then, they opened their treasures and presented Him with the most precious gifts that they had—gold, frankincense, and myrrh. It would have been unthinkable for them to worship the Lord without giving Him gifts.

In 2 Corinthians 8, we see poor Christians going beyond themselves to give. Verse five says that they first gave themselves to the Lord, and then they gave of their finances. Financial giving, properly understood, is first an act of worship to the Lord. We demonstrate our reverence and honor for Him by sacrificing to Him something of worth.

Scripture teaches us four principles of giving:

1. The Stewardship Principle: God owns everything. I am merely an assets manager.

Haggai 2:8 tells us, "The silver is Mine and the gold is Mine." Deuteronomy 8:18 reminds us, "Remember the LORD your God, for it is He who is giving you power to make wealth."

So, it is clear that the One who created gold does not need our gold. His asking us to be generous and faithful in our giving is a test to measure our commitment to Him and to eternal things (2 Cor. 8–9). It is also a test of our readiness to trust Him to meet our needs as He has promised He would do (Matt. 6).

2. The Treasure Principle: We cannot take it with us, but we can send it ahead.

In his valuable book *The Treasure Principle*,[2] Randy Alcorn makes this important point. Send it ahead. Store up your treasures in heaven.

Jesus said in Matthew 6:19–21, "Do not store up for yourselves treasures on earth, where moth and rust destroy, and where thieves break in and steal. But store up for yourselves treasures in heaven, where neither moth nor rust destroys, and where thieves do not break in or steal; for where your treasure is, there your heart will be also."

Jim Elliot, a missionary to Ecuador in the mid-twentieth century, wrote in his diary not long before he was killed by the Auca Indians he was trying to reach for the gospel, "He is no fool who gives up that which he cannot keep to gain that which he cannot lose." [3]

3. The Giving Principle: You only keep what you give away.

Scripture teaches that eternal wealth is gained by doing good in this life. In 1 Corinthians 3:14, we read that as a result of doing good works, "if any man's work which he has built on [the foundation of Jesus Christ] remains, he will receive a reward."

Jesus is keeping track of our smallest acts of kindness. "And whoever in the name of a disciple gives to one of these little ones even a cup of cold water to drink, truly I say to you, he shall not lose his reward" (Matt. 10:42).

God is keeping a record of all we do for Him. The Old Testament prophet Malachi wrote, "A book of remembrance was written before Him for those who fear the LORD and who esteem His name" (Mal. 3:16).

Imagine a scribe in heaven recording each of your gifts in that book. The bike you gave to the neighbor kid, the meal you took to a sick person, the checks you write to the church, missionaries, those in need—all are being chronicled.

Nothing that we spend on ourselves for personal gain translates into eternal reward. We only keep what we give away.

4. The Source Principle: God wants us to view Him as the source of all our money and give accordingly.

The Lord wants us to view ourselves as conduits for His resources, rather than seeing ourselves as reservoirs of our own resources. If we see ourselves as conduits of God's reservoir of resources, we will be less inclined to hoard our resources, and more inclined to pass them on, believing that God will take care of us as we do.

Paul says as much in Philippians 4. He thanks the Philippians for their generosity in meeting his needs as he was traveling in ministry. Then he adds in verse nineteen, "My God will supply all your needs according to His riches in glory in Christ Jesus." The Philippians were a conduit to flow God's resources to Paul, and, in return, God would meet their needs.

Paul reinforced this principle in 2 Corinthians 9 when he wrote, "He who sows sparingly will also reap sparingly, and he who sows bountifully will also reap bountifully. . . . And God is able to make all grace abound to you, so that always having all sufficiency in everything, you may have an abundance for every good deed" (vv. 6, 8).

God will give us all the money we need to do all the good works He wants us to do. I do not think that means we can be foolish and shovel money away that God may intend to meet our own needs. But it does mean that we can be open to God's leading to give money away, because if He does, He will meet our needs at the same time. We will have all the money we need to do all the good works God calls us to.

The principle from the 2 Corinthians 9 passage is that if we view ourselves as conduits for His resources, He will funnel through us money that He wants to go to other needs. In doing so, He meets needs of others through us, He meets our needs as well, our faith is stretched, and our joy is increased.

Conclusion

Christians commit to a local congregation to honor the spirit of Scripture. So, find the best church you can and commit to it, and try to make that church better. In his book *In, but Not Of*, Hugh Hewitt wrote of this:

> Choosing a church home is not as difficult as choosing a spouse, but it can and often does have as much impact on your life as your mate will. If you take church seriously, it will absorb a large portion of your life and will inevitably shape your weeks, months, and years. A genuine commitment to a congregation of believers is a massive undertaking. Whether you have just arrived in a city or town, or whether you have been there for some years, look around for a vibrant faith community and go there. Join it. Dive into it. No piece of advice I give is more valuable than this one.[4]

Christians are family and should care for one another. Therefore, the sixth mark of a complete Christian is that he impacts the church.

Review for Memory

1. Christians are f _amily_ and should care for one another. (Page 94)

2. Christians serve the L _ord_ by serving the c _hurch_ . (Page 89)

3. Christians serve the church with their t _ime_ and t _alents_ . (Page 89)

4. Christians serve the church with their t _reasure_ . (Page 91)

5. There are four biblical principles of giving:
   a. The S _tewardship_ Principle
   b. The T _reasure_ Principle
   c. The G _iving_ Principle
   d. The S _ource_ Principle (Pages 91–94)

Review for Understanding

Summarize in one paragraph what you think the most important message of this chapter is:

A major responsibility we have as Christians is to serve the church with our time, treasure and talents. The way we treat the church is actually how we are treating Jesus.

Review for Application

Write out how you think that knowing this will influence your Christian impact in the church:

I intend to serve faithfully, at Calvary and be involved in my small group. I also want to meet others' needs and tithe faithfully.

CHAPTER 10

Central Passage: *"As You sent Me into the world,*
I also have sent them into the world" (John 17:18).

Mark No. 7: A Complete Christian Impacts the World

Because God loved the world and gave Himself for it, so should we. Therefore, a complete Christian serves the world through evangelism and humanitarianism.

In the book entitled *What If Jesus Had Never Been Born?*[1] D. James Kennedy detailed the contribution of Christianity to the world. It is a powerful and enlightening book. With careful historical research, he demonstrated that true Christianity has been responsible for major contributions to civilization that are often overlooked or taken for granted, including:

1. **Valuing human life.** Prior to the coming of Christ, human life was very cheap. Christianity has championed the value and welfare of the unborn, children, women, the elderly, and the disabled—leading the way to provide them protection and dignity.

2. **Helping the poor.** Before the coming of Christianity, there is no evidence of any organized effort to help the poor. Instead, the poor were considered a resource to exploit for the benefit of the wealthy. It was astonishing to the first-century observers that

Christians helped one another and helped those who could not help themselves.

3. **Providing literacy for everyone.** Christianity gave rise to the concept of education for everyone. Christians desired for everyone to be able to read the Word of God in their own language. That led to many languages being written down. Then the printing press was invented, and children were taught to read—creating a largely literate world.

4. **The expansion of democracy.** Christianity fueled the concept of democratic government, believing that "all men are created equal, that they are endowed by their Creator with certain unalienable Rights," and that the purpose of government was to protect those rights.

5. **The advancement of civil liberties.** Christianity led the charge against slavery—starting in England and America and continuing around the world. It has stood for the equal treatment of all minorities. While there have been examples of those claiming Christ who have not advanced civil liberties and equal treatment for all, they were not following the clear teachings of Christ who taught that we should love our neighbors as ourselves.

6. **The advancement of science.** We live, unquestionably, in an age of science. Many scholars agree that the scientific revolution was birthed for the most part by Christians because of the medieval insistence on the "rationality of God," as historian Alfred North Whitehead put it.[2] If Jesus had never been born, science as we know it would likely not have come into being.

7. **The advancement of health and medicine.** Compassion for others is inherent to true Christianity. This has led to the advancement of medicine and medical treatment on a scale that would have otherwise been unlikely. Before Christianity, medical

treatment was considered a privilege reserved for the wealthy who could afford to pay for it.

8. **The creation and promotion of great art.** Art has been seen as a means of expressing praise and worship to God; and, as a result, Christianity has had a profound impact on great art— from the architecture of great cathedrals to music, literature, and visual arts.

Beyond D. James Kennedy, many scholars have demonstrated that Christianity has given the world the gift of the dignity and worth of the individual, the gift of science, the gift of literacy, the gift of humility, the compassionate use of power, and many other values that have shaped civilization for the better.[3]

Scripture makes it clear that reaching out to the world was a top priority of Jesus when He was here on earth, and He passed that priority down to all His followers. In John 17:18, Jesus said a profound prayer to the heavenly Father, "As You sent Me into the world, I also have sent [my disciples] into the world."

Jesus made a historic impact on the world through His followers who took His teachings to their logical conclusion in their time and place. That is what Jesus wants from all of us—**to take His teachings to their logical conclusion in our time and place**.

There are two primary ways we do this. First, we evangelize, addressing the eternal needs of humanity, and second, we are humanitarian, addressing the temporal needs of humanity.

Christians Evangelize to Address the Eternal Needs of Humanity

In Matthew 28:19–20, we read, "Go therefore and make disciples of all the nations, baptizing them in the name of the Father and the Son and the Holy Spirit, teaching them to observe all that I commanded you; and lo, I am with you always, even to the end of the age."

This is often called the Great Commission. A commission is a job, a task. When cadets graduate from military academies, they are given a commission—that is, a position and task. Sometimes artists and composers are given a commission to paint a picture or write a musical piece. A commission is something we are given to do. And just before Jesus left this earth, after He was crucified and resurrected, He gave each of us a commission, a task, a responsibility to go into all the world and make disciples of all the nations.

This is the first great responsibility of the church, and of each individual Christian to play his or her intended role in the pursuit of this commission. The task is great, and the need is urgent.

In order to have sufficient motivation to evangelize, we must be persuaded that the need is real, that people are lost unless they receive the gospel. When we become sufficiently persuaded of this fundamental biblical doctrine, we set our hearts and minds to do what Christ calls us to. A story is often told of the impact of hell on some American soldiers:

> The military chaplain didn't believe in Hell. He was surprised to learn that it made a big difference to the soldiers he was sent to minister to. A group of servicemen had a new chaplain appointed to them. The soldiers were not Christians, and they wondered what kind of religion this fellow really had. They approached the new chaplain and said, "Tell us, do you believe in a real Hell?"
>
> "A literal Hell?" the chaplain asked.
>
> "Yes, that's the one," one of them answered.
>
> The chaplain, who held a liberal view of Scripture said, "No, rest assured, boys, I don't believe in a literal Hell."
>
> He thought this would make them happy. But their response caught him off guard. They said, "Well, then, you're wasting your time and our time, because if there is no Hell, we don't need you. But if there is a Hell, you're leading us astray. Either way, we're better off without you."[4]

Evangelism is a top priority for a complete Christian because the lost are lost, and Jesus commands us to take the gospel to the lost.

Often, Christians are not sufficiently involved in evangelism because they have been intimidated into thinking that they have to evangelize the way someone else thinks they should evangelize, as we saw in chapter 8. In addition, we are often intimidated by social factors. We may be so busy that we have trouble knowing or caring about anything not on our over-full to-do list. Other times, we are afraid or embarrassed to share our faith and risk rejection or ridicule. Or, we may get lulled into thinking that someone else will evangelize lost people. Finally, we may be unsure if someone we think is lost is really lost.

Yet all these mental obstacles are things the Enemy uses to neutralize us and keep us from evangelizing. The reality is, God does not need us to evangelize. He can use someone else to reach a person if we will not. And now, after the turn of the century, we are hearing amazing tales from Muslim countries of Jesus revealing Himself in visions and dreams to individuals and thousands are coming to Christ without a human evangelist.

> God does not need us to evangelize to accomplish His purposes. But we need to evangelize.

So, God does not need us to evangelize to accomplish His purposes. But we need to evangelize. When we become mature in Christ, we will evangelize. If we are not evangelizing, we are not yet mature in that area of spiritual growth. So, the great issue in evangelizing is that God gives us the privilege of being used by Him to usher human souls into eternity. It is something we all should aspire to.

The first step in spiritual growth regarding evangelism is to accept the Great Commission as our own personal commission. It is possible to see the Great Commission just as something for international missionaries or people who do not have more valuable things to do with their lives. A careful reading of the Scripture, however, makes it clear that each of us is to embrace the Great Commission as our own commission and be committed to playing whatever role God asks of us in the pursuit of it.

Scripture teaches that some people are spiritually gifted to evangelize (Eph. 4:11). This means, of course, that others are not. Those who are spiritually gifted to evangelize will have strong motivation and greater-than-average effectiveness. Nevertheless, even those who are not spiritually gifted in that area are responsible to evangelize. The apostle Paul instructed his young disciple Timothy, who was gifted as a pastor, to "do the work of an evangelist" (2 Tim. 4:5).

The point is, regardless of whether or not we have the gift of evangelism, we are all to do the work of evangelism. A complete Christian must accept that this commission is not just for someone else.

Christians Are Humanitarian to Address the Temporal Needs of Humanity

In addition to evangelism, Jesus commanded us to help meet the needs of this life, to help make the world a better place in which to live, to reduce human suffering, and to prepare hearts to receive the gospel.

James 2:15–17 says, "If a brother or sister is without clothing and in need of daily food, and one of you says to them, 'Go in peace, be warmed and be filled,' and yet you do not give them what is necessary for *their* body, what use is that? Even so faith, if it has no works, is dead, *being* by itself." We see Jesus throughout the Gospels meeting people's physical needs and then sharing the gospel with them. The two go hand in hand.

Humanitarianism helps make the world a better place in which to live, and it prepares hearts to receive the gospel. Luke 6:31, which says, "Treat others the same way you want them to treat you," is a great passage to move us out of our comfort zone. Just ask yourself what you would want others to do for you if you were in their shoes.

When we help others in need, we help make the world a better place in which to live. When we support Habitat for Humanity, when we support agricultural initiatives in Africa, when we contribute to an orphanage in South America, we help make the world a better place in which to live, and we fulfill Jesus' command to "treat others the same way you want them to treat you." Of course, we cannot meet all the needs. Even the richest person in the world does not have enough money to meet everyone's needs. But we can do what we believe the Lord wants us to do.

As we saw earlier, there are two reasons why we should be involved in humanitarianism. One is in order to help make the world a better place in which to live. The other is that it also helps prepare people's hearts to hear the gospel. This follows Jesus' pattern. He often met people's physical needs and then shared the gospel with them. For us to engage in both evangelism and humanitarianism makes us more complete Christians and helps meet the critical needs that exist in the world around us, both for time and eternity. It is a good and right thing to do.

Conclusion

Historically, conservative churches have tended to emphasize evangelism over humanitarianism, while liberal churches have tended to emphasize humanitarianism over evangelism. **However, like two wings of an airplane, the complete Christian must be committed to both.**

Ministering to the world can be a daunting challenge for some Christians. The needs are so intimidating, it requires such a major departure from our comfort zone, and the needs are so overwhelming, we can wonder what difference it makes whether we get involved or not.

An often told story is of a man who was staying at an ocean-side hotel where he was conducting a seminar. Early one morning, he went out on the beach and saw a young man throwing starfish back into the water. Some tide condition had washed them up by the thousands. After watching for a while, the older man walked out and said, "Why are you bothering to throw those starfish back into the water? There are so many of them, you can't possibly make a difference." The young man looked at him, looked at the starfish in his hand, and as he threw the starfish back into the ocean, he said, "It made a difference to that one."

When addressing world hunger, for example, we cannot feed everyone, but if each of us feeds one, that will mean that considerably fewer people will go hungry. That is the perspective we must have. We must focus on individuals, not masses. If we try to absorb the magnitude of the masses, we may get overwhelmed. But if we focus on one individual, we can rest assured that whatever we do makes a big difference to that one.

Because God loved the world and gave Himself for it, so should we. Therefore, the seventh mark of a complete Christian is that he impacts the world through evangelism and humanitarianism.

Review for Memory

1. Jesus wants each of us to take His teachings to their l _ogical_ c _onclusion_ in our time and place. (Page 99)

2. Christians e _vangelize_ to address the e _ternal_ needs of humanity. (Page 99)

3. Christians are h _umanitarian_ to address the t _emporal_ needs of humanity. (Page 102)

4. Like two wings of an airplane, a complete Christian must be committed to both e *vangelism* and h *umanitarianism* (Page 103)

Review for Understanding

Summarize in one paragraph what you think the most important message of this chapter is:

Christians ought to meet people's eternal and temporal needs for the sake of the gospel. This looks like evangelism and humanitarianism. Both are needed.

Review for Application

Write out how you think that knowing this will influence your Christian impact in the world:

I need to be more intentional to meet others' temporal needs.

CHAPTER 11

Central Passage: "We proclaim Him, admonishing every man and teaching every man with all wisdom, so that we may present every man complete in Christ" (Col. 1:28).

The Seven Ministries of a Complete Church

The seven marks of a complete Christian mandate, by default, seven ministries of a complete church.

S ince the mandate of the local church is to present its members complete in Christ, the seven marks of a complete Christian that we overviewed in the pervious seven chapters become, by default, the seven ministries of a complete church.

In Colossians 1:28 the apostle Paul wrote, "We proclaim Him, admonishing every man and teaching every man with all wisdom, so that we may *present every man complete in Christ*" (italics added for emphasis). So this passage establishes the responsibility of the church to help its members become complete in their spiritual growth.

The word for *complete* in this passage is from the Greek word in the Bible, *teleos*, which means mature, fully formed, complete. When a farmer plants a kernel of corn, that kernel sprouts, puts down roots, and shoots up a stalk. Then, the stalk produces an ear that has many kernels on it. When all the kernels on the new ear are fully formed and the ear of corn is harvested, that original seed is said to be *teleos*, or mature, complete. The reason for its having been planted is fully realized. That is the idea of *teleos*. Paul says that his goal is to present every person *teleos* in Christ—complete, mature, fully formed.

Therefore, each of the seven marks of a complete Christian is a need that the individual has if he or she is to be complete in Christ, and those needs give rise to the mandate of a complete church. If the individual's need is to worship God individually, then the responsibility of the church is to facilitate individual worship. If the need of the individual is to worship God corporately, then the responsibility of the church is to inspire corporate worship, and so on. The following represents this link between individual needs and church responsibilities succinctly in chart form:

Individual Need:	**Church Responsibility:**
If the individual's need is . . .	*Then the church's responsibility is to . . .*
. . . individual worship	. . . facilitate individual worship
. . . corporate worship	. . . inspire corporate worship
. . . growth in biblical knowledge	. . . instruct in biblical knowledge
. . . growth in Christlike lifestyle	. . . nurture Christlike lifestyle
. . . growth in ministry skill	. . . train in ministry skill
. . . impact the church	. . . mobilize for impacting the church
. . . impact the world	. . . deploy for impacting the world

The default seven ministries of a complete church, then, are to:

1. **facilitate** individual worship,

2. **inspire** corporate worship,

3. **instruct** in biblical knowledge,

4. **nurture** Christlike lifestyle,

5. **train** in ministry skill,

6. **mobilize** for impacting the church, and

7. **deploy** for impacting the world.

The mandate of the church regarding its members, then, can be reduced to seven words: facilitate, inspire, instruct, nurture, train, mobilize, and deploy.

We saw in chapter 3 that when these seven needs/responsibilities are boiled down to their irreducible minimum, there are three:

1. Worship
   a. Individually
   b. Corporately

2. Grow
   a. Biblical knowledge
   b. Christlike lifestyle
   c. Ministry skill

3. Impact
   a. Church
   b. World

Of these three, worship and impact are different from grow. Individual worship and corporate worship are things that can be planned, scheduled, and completed. That is, you can have a time of personal devotion each morning and attend church each Sunday, and you will have fulfilled your responsibility that week for worship. You can give time, talent, and treasure to the church and can contribute to humanitarian needs as well as share your faith, and you will have fulfilled your responsibility as best you can that week. But growth is not something that can be checked off a list. It is something that has to be pursued on an ever-increasing level the rest of one's life. There-fore, the grow category must be given an ongoing level of attention far beyond worship and impact. It is more time consuming and less easy to measure.

Beyond that, there are methodology issues that affect these matters. The three categories that growth breaks down into each have their own ministry methods that must be used if each of the three ministry goals is to be achieved.

Growth is made up of the know, be, and do components:

▶ Know = must use knowledge methods

▶ Be = must use lifestyle change methods

▶ Do = must use ministry skill acquisition methods

As we will see in the coming chapters, educational research plus examples from Scripture and common sense tell us that each of these ministry goals must be accomplished with different ministry methods. That is, if you want to help a person grow in his knowledge of the Bible, it takes one set of methods. If you want to help a person grow in his character and Christlike lifestyle, there is a second set of methods that must be used. If you want to help a person grow in his ministry skill, there is a third set of methods that must be used.

. . . each of these ministry goals must be accomplished with different ministry methods.

And, as we will see, these methods do not cross over. That is, knowledge methods do not readily achieve lifestyle goals. Lifestyle methods do not readily achieve ministry skill goals, and so on. Therefore, specific additional attention must be given to the methodology attached to the know-be-do triad if we want to be effective in translating our hard ministry work into results.

In addition, compared to the church's task of helping Christians grow to maturity in Christ, it is comparatively easy to help them worship God and get involved in ministry. **The hard part—the very, very hard part—is to help them grow to spiritual maturity in Christ.**

As a result, the three ministry goals of (1) helping a person grow in biblical knowledge, (2) growing in Christlike lifestyle, and (3) growing in ministry skill must be singled out and given much additional attention. A major purpose of this book is to communicate that we must give specific attention to these three areas and what ministry methods must be used to address them. We will take up that task in the next chapter.

Review for Memory

1. The seven m *arks* of a complete Christian mandate the default seven m *inistries* of a complete church. (Page 107)

2. The seven ministries of a complete church are:
   a. F *acilitate* individual worship,
   b. I *nspire* corporate worship,
   c. I *nstruct* in biblical knowledge,
   d. N *urture* Christlike lifestyle,
   e. T *rain* in ministry skill,
   f. M *obilize* for impacting the church, and
   g. D *eploy* for impacting the world. (Pages 108–9)

3. It is comparatively easy to help a person worship and minister. The very hard part is to help them grow to s *piritual* m *aturity* in Christ. (Page 111)

Review for Understanding

Summarize in one paragraph what you think the most important message of this chapter is:

The church has the responsibility to use different ministry methods to help believers grow in the 7 areas of mature christians. The end goal for the church is to produce mature believers.

Review for Application

Write out how you think that knowing this will influence your Christian impact in the world:

It is good to consider these areas, but honestly this chapter focuses mostly on those in church leadership. I could raise awareness in my church for the need to incorporate different ministries that are lacking, but that's it.

Central Passage: *"For Ezra had set his heart to study the law of the* Lord*, and to practice it, and to teach His statutes and ordinances in Israel" (Ezra 7:10).*

The Three Spiritual Growth Goals

There are three, and only three, educational goals leading to spiritual growth.

This brings us to elaborating on the point made in the last chapter. Two of the needs of a Christian, worship and impact, are comparatively easy. The bigger job is the need to grow in the three areas of knowledge, lifestyle, and ministry skill. These three areas from Ezra 7:10 form the triad of major discipleship challenge. **Each Christian needs to grow to maturity in what he knows, how he lives, and what he can do, and the church is responsible to help him succeed.**

It was a revelation when I learned this in seminary at the feet of Dr. Hendricks, perhaps the greatest Christian teacher of the last generation. A few years later, a second dawning occurred. I had been exposed to some classic, educational research resources as I was completing my master's degree in Christian education,[1] and I was keenly interested in how to teach effectively. I had already been inoculated against boring and ineffective teaching from early teaching failures as a young Christian college instructor. I was also teaching Walk Thru the Bible seminars at the time, wildly creative Bible-teaching experiences that turned traditional biblical instruction on its head for me and made my imagination dance with possibilities for more effective instruction. One day, I added *Design for Teaching and Training* by Leroy Ford[2] to my educational resource bank and finally came to grasp that there are basically three educational goals:

1. You can impart knowledge and information to people and <u>help them learn to think.</u> *He values this more than Smith*

2. You can influence their attitudes, values, and behavior.

3. You can teach them a skill.

Of course, these three goals are presaged by the very titles of the taxonomy research projects: cognitive domain (know), affective domain (be), and psychomotor domain (do), but I had not seen the forest for the trees.

As I pondered the correlation between Ezra 7:10 (know-be-do) and the contribution of educational research (knowledge-behavior-skill), a shaft of sunlight beamed down on me from somewhere on high. Flowers bloomed suddenly. Birds warbled nearby. Angels sang softly in the background.

. . . educational research-ers had observed what methods were most helpful to help people know, be and do what the Bible says.

Over a period of time, it began to dawn on me that educational researchers had observed what methods were most helpful to help people know, be, and do what the Bible says. If I wanted to help a person gain biblical knowledge, educational research shed light on the best ways to do it. If I wanted to help a person grow in his Christian character and lifestyle, educational research shed light on the best ways to do it. If I wanted to help a person learn how to gain the ministry skills needed to successfully use his spiritual gifts, educational research shed light on the best ways do it.

It was too good to be true.

Instead of groping around in the dark, instead of doing unto others what others had done unto me, instead of experimenting on my students to see what worked and what did not, I now had a methodology blueprint that told me how to do each of the three things I wanted to do for the people I was ministering to. A new day dawned.

I now understood that if I wanted to impart biblical information as effectively as possible, I had to conform to the laws of learning knowledge that God had created. I also had to conform to the laws that God created if I wanted to impact a person's lifestyle. And finally, I had to do the same if I wanted to impart a skill. God does not override the laws by which He created us to learn, grow, and function, just as He does not override the laws of science and nature. We are no wiser to ignore these laws of learning than we would be to ignore the law of gravity. He uses those laws, and a world of possibilities opens to us when we follow them.

Said another way, each of the three central ministry goals—knowledge, lifestyle, or ministry skill—has its own separate and distinct methodology that must be employed if the goal is to be optimally achieved. Knowledge goals require different methodology than lifestyle goals, and lifestyle goals require different methodology than skill goals.

For a *knowledge* goal you must use . . .	For a *lifestyle* goal you must use . . .	For a ministry *skill* goal you must use . . .
▼	▼	▼
knowledge methods	*lifestyle* methods	*skill* methods

Remember, the methods do not cross purposes. That is, knowledge methods do not readily achieve lifestyle goals. Lifestyle methods do not readily achieve skill goals, and so on. So, the right material must be taught but also in the right way.

He sees value in all three

▶ The *knowledge* goals require methodology that is often seen better in classrooms. These goals might be easily reached in a Sunday school environment, small group environment, or seminar environment.

▶ The *lifestyle* goals require some typical education methodology, but the most powerful lifestyle impact is made life-on-life through modeling and mentoring.

▶ Finally, the *skill* goals are best achieved in an environment that approximates or replicates the skill. That is, if you want to train a person to fly a helicopter, you must do so from the helicopter. In ministry settings, if you want to train a person to be able to teach, it must include a teaching environment. If you want to train a person to be able to counsel, it must include counseling situations. It cannot be done exclusively in a classroom.

This book will eventually go into greater detail regarding these distinctions, but the first step is understanding that the distinctions exist.

	Knowledge Goals	Lifestyle Goals	Ministry Skill Goals
Discipleship Venue	Classroom-type environment	Relationship-based environment	Internship-type environment

Understanding this, we can explore a strategy to help a person know what he needs to know, become what he needs to be, and do what he needs to do. We can start by asking three questions:

	Know	Be	Do
Christian	What should a Christian know?	What should a Christian be?	What should a Christian do?

These are very simple questions, and yet very few people have a solid answer to these questions. To be able to answer these questions is to possess a power that few possess. It is the power of goals. If you are clear on what you want to do, you are halfway toward being able to do it. If you are not clear on what you want to do, you grope, you experiment, and you shoot in the dark. Answering these questions is simple—but difficult. It requires both a depth of biblical knowledge and a wealth of ministry experience. The better we understand this, the more potential we have to make a complete impact in a person's life.

Then, if you are a pastor responsible for all age groups in your church, you must ask the question of each of the age groups. There are three major age groups in a local church: adults, youth, and children. Each age has needs for knowledge, lifestyle, and ministry skills on a level that is appropriate to the age. The following chart helps us see this at a glance:

Know–Be–Do All-Church Strategy

	Know	Be	Do
Adult	What does an *adult* need to *know*?	What does an *adult* need to *be*?	What does an *adult* need to *do*?
Youth	What do *youth* need to *know*?	What do *youth* need to *be*?	What do *youth* need to *do*?
Children	What do *children* need to *know*?	What do *children* need to *be*?	What do *children* need to *do*?

This chart illustrates the profound and deeply leading question, What does an adult need to know, be, and do? Because of age-level characteristics, the answer to that question is different from the second question, What does a youth need to know, be, and do? And this is different from the third question, What does a child need to know, be, and do? What we expect a youth to know is less than we expect an adult to know. And what we expect a child to know is less than a youth. So, each question must be asked and answered for the specific age category. This chart enables the local church to be fairly specific in creating a cradle-to-grave curriculum strategy for discipling its people to maturity in Christ.

It is not within the scope of this book to give a detailed answer to the questions of what a Christian needs to know, be, and do. In fact, it is generally only educators and curriculum writers who go through the very exacting discipline of identifying specifics of what each of these age groups need to know, be, and do. However, it is very helpful to have general guidelines to use to guide our own ministry as well as to select curriculum for various ministry settings.

Know

For a number of years, I taught as an adjunct faculty member in several theological seminaries. During that time, I asked hundreds of students the question, "If a person 'knows' the Bible, what does he know?" After asking that question, I would write furiously on a chalk/white board the answers that the students suggested. We would often end up with dozens of words defining an aspect of what a person would know if he knew the Bible. The suggestions always fell into three broad categories, as I said in an earlier chapter. However, they were also easily divided into five more specific ones.

1. **Facts**: If a person knows the Bible, he knows the people, places, events, and chronology of the Bible story.

2. **Doctrines**: If a person knows the Bible, he knows what the Bible teaches about God, Christ, the Holy Spirit, angels/demons, man-sin-salvation, the church, and future things.

3. **Principles**: If a person knows the Bible, he knows principles of Christian living, how to pray, how to discern God's will, how to walk in the spirit, and how to live the Christian life.

4. **Problems**: If a person knows the Bible, he knows how its truth applies to specific problems he may be facing such as peer pressure, husband/wife relationships, child-rearing issues, anger, fear, depression, moral purity, and so on.

5. **Apologetics**: If a person knows the Bible, he knows how to defend his faith from falsehood, attacks, and unbelief.

Be

Ascertaining what a person should be is more abstract. Yet on its broadest scale, Scripture makes it clear that love is a central character trait, both for God and for His children. Our lifestyles are to be marked with love. In fact, in Matthew 22:37–40, Jesus said the greatest command is to love the Lord your God with all your heart, soul, and mind, and that the second greatest command is to love your neighbor as yourself. He explained that on these two commandments depended the whole law and the prophets. That is, the law and the prophets explained in specific detail how we are to go about loving God and our neighbor.

So, **love is the key lifestyle attribute that Christians are to take on**.

While that observation is helpful, if we get one level more specific, it will help put legs on the idea, because our instinctive first question is, What does it mean to love God, and what does it meant to love my neighbor? Specifically, how do I go about it? There are two helpful answers to that question.

Concerning loving God, in John 14:15 it says, "If you love Me, you will keep My commandments." So, a spirit of trust and obedience to God's commandments is a foundational concept in loving God. This may seem obvious, but it is central, nevertheless. If we love God, we trust Him. If we trust Him, we obey Him. If we do not obey Him, we do not yet trust Him. If we do not trust Him, we do not yet love Him.

There are three different postures of Christians toward this idea.

1. We love, trust, and obey God in all things.

2. We love, trust, and obey God in some things.

3. We love, trust, and obey God in nothing.

Most Christians are in category two, hopefully headed in the direction of category one.

Concerning loving our neighbor, 1 Corinthians 13:4–8 says:

> Love is patient, love is kind *and* is not jealous; love does not brag *and* is not arrogant, does not act unbecomingly; it does not seek its own, is not provoked, does not take into account a wrong *suffered*, does not rejoice in unrighteousness, but rejoices with the truth; bears all things, believes all things, hopes all things, endures all things. Love never fails.

This passage, then, becomes a guiding light for what it means to love our neighbor as ourselves. When we take on these lifestyle characteristics of patience, kindness, unselfishness, forgiveness, and so on, we fulfill the second great commandment to love our neighbor. In essence, we love our neighbor as we treat him as we would want to be treated.

The specific application for love must be age-appropriate. We might want a first-grader merely to learn to say please and thank you and be willing to share. However, a person who has been a Christian for a long time should be challenged to forgive when wronged, to give up on anger, to take on selflessness.

So, as we ask the question, What does a Christian need to be? we answer that he needs to be someone who loves God and demonstrates that love by trusting and obeying Him, and we love our neighbor by treating him as we would want to be treated.

Do

Determining what we should do is related to our responsibilities to share our faith and use our spiritual gifts. So, on an age-appropriate level, **a person should be trained in how to share his faith and how to use his spiritual gift(s)**. This will have to be very basic for younger children and will be advanced for mature Christians.

Most disciplers are not prepared to write their own curriculum to make sure these truths are represented on an age-appropriate level. However, it is essential to evaluate curriculum that may be being used, to make sure that, over the long haul, these three know-be-do goals are addressed for all age groups for which you are responsible.

To summarize, then, we see that there are three, and only three, basic goals in spiritual growth: to learn what we need to know, become what we were meant to be, and do what we were meant to be. As we are clear on these three goals, we are able to direct our ministries to accomplish these goals in the lives of others.

However, there is another critical link in this process. That is, we must use the right methods for the ministry goal. That is, educational research tells us that if we want to teach someone knowledge, there are certain methods we must use. The same is true for lifestyle and ministry skill. As we said, we are no wiser to ignore these laws than if we were to ignore the law of gravity. Therefore, we turn our attention in the next chapter to identifying these ministry methods.

Get ready. This is where rubber meets the road!

> So, on an age-appropriate level, a person should be trained in how to share his faith and how to use his spiritual gift(s).

Review for Memory

1. There are t _lnee_ educational goals leading to spiritual g _nowth_ . (Page 113)

2. Each Christian needs to grow to maturity in what he k _nows_ , how he l _iver_ , and what he can d _do_ , and the church is responsible to help him succeed. (Page 113)

3. Concerning the discipleship venue,
   a. Knowledge goals are best achieved in a c _lassroom_ -type environment.
   b. Lifestyle goals are best achieved in a r _elationship_ -based environment.
   c. Skill goals are best achieved in an i _nternship_ -type environment. (Page 116)

4. If a person knows the Bible, he knows the
   a. F _acts_ ,
   b. D _octrine_ , and
   c. P _rinciples_ of Christian living in the Bible (Page 118–119)

5. L _ove_ is the key lifestyle attribute that Christians are to take on. (Page 119)

6. A Christian is responsible to learn how to share his f _aith_ and use his s _piritual_ g _ifts_ . (Page 121)

Review for Understanding

Summarize in one paragraph what you think the most important message of this chapter is:

There are 3 educational goals for Christians: know, be, do, and each requires specific methods and contexts to be taught effectively.

Review for Application

Write out how you think that knowing this will influence your Christian impact in the world:

I really liked the point about lifestyle goals being best achieved in relationship. It helps give me a better perspective on discipleship and the goals/outcomes to aim for in that.

CHAPTER 13

Central Passage: *"You will know the truth,*
and the truth will make you free" (John 8:32).

Knowledge Methods Must Match Knowledge Goals

To help a Christian master what he needs to know, knowledge methods must be used.

As we have seen there are three ministry goals. We can teach for **knowledge**, we can teach for **lifestyle**, or we can teach for **ministry skill**. Everything we hope to accomplish in personal growth falls into one of these three major categories.

In addition, we have seen that each of these three ministry goals has its own set of methods that must be employed if the goal is to be reached. It is now time to look at those methods. As I have studied the relationship between methods and goals, it has become clear that there is no fixed and absolute list of methods. But there is a clear trend in the methods. As we saw earlier, knowledge methods tend to include those that are seen better in classrooms. Lifestyle methods tend to include personal relationships and lifestyle-modeling. Skill-acquisition methods tend to include demonstrations and rehearsal.

However, when you are down in the trenches actually discipling people or teaching something, it is valuable to look at some specific methods. The methods that I will be suggesting were forged out of a number of years of study when getting my master's degree and doctorate, plus over thirty years of ministry experience. I used these methods when helping finalize content for Walk Thru the Bible seminars, when teaching in college and in seminaries, when writing my book *30 Days to Understanding the Bible* and other books, when creating the template for the thirty-two-volume Holman Bible Commentary series for which I was creator and general editor, and in over twenty-five years of pastoring and discipling in local churches.

If someone were reading or taking a course on educational methodology, this information would be much more complex and thorough, but experience has led me to believe that less is more in this case and that it is better for learners to get all of a little rather than none of a lot. So I have boiled this information down to its irreducible minimum and have found that non-educators are able to profit from the information more easily as a result.

This chapter will focus on teaching for knowledge and will look more closely at the methods that need to be employed if we want to conform to how God created us to gain knowledge.

Knowledge is a large category that, unlike lifestyle and skill, is divided into subcategories. Educators identify as many as six different levels of knowledge. However, I have become convinced that it is most helpful to focus on just three. In my experience they are the ones that are most usable in a ministry setting, and getting more specific often overwhelms those for whom this is new territory:

1. **Memory**: being able to remember what has been taught.

2. **Understanding**: being able to comprehend what has been taught.

3. **Application**: being able to apply what is taught in one's own life and/or ministry.

Each of these three levels of knowledge has its own methodology that must be used if the ministry goal is to be realized.

Memory: The Ability to Recall What Has Been Taught

When teaching for memory, the following methods are effective:

▶ **Reduction**   ▶ **Creativity**

▶ **Preview**   ▶ **Multiplicity**

▶ **Activity**   ▶ **Feedback**

▶ **Progressivity**   ▶ **Repetition**

Reduction

A 1982 study conducted by Carnegie-Mellon University (*Memory and Cognition*)[1] demonstrated that a learner retains more from a tight condensation of a book than if he reads the whole book. This suggests that, to aid memorization, we can boil the material down to its irreducible minimum so that the learner only has to memorize the irreducible minimum and not the whole body of information. As an example, a tight outline of a subject is often the most helpful format for memorizing material under the conviction that it is better to remember all of a little than none of a lot.

. . . a learner retains more from a tight condensation of a book than if he reads the whole book.

Walk Thru the Bible Ministries was begun as a seminar ministry designed to give people an overview of the Old and New Testaments in two separate all-day seminars. As one of the original team members of Walk thru the Bible Ministries, I was involved in the final process of assessing what content would be included in the first generation of seminars. Clearly, we could not teach everything about each of the

Testaments in a single day, so we undertook the task of deciding what would be left in and what would be left out. In the end, we created an outline of each Testament, highlighting the major men and women, the major events, and the major locations, and put them together in their chronological order and geographic location to tell the story of the Bible as completely as we could in a single-day seminar.

When the seminar was over, the audience could, with the leadership of the seminar instructor, recite a concise summary of the Old or New Testament from memory. It was a powerful and often life-changing experience for some people, myself included. Very creative teaching-for-memory methodology was employed to enable people to recall more than they ever thought possible at the beginning of the day. But the first principle employed was the principle of reduction: boiling the material down to its irreducible minimum so that all that was memorized was that basic core of information.

A powerful side benefit, however, is that when people want to retrieve the memorized outline from their memory bank, they can retrieve not only the concise outline that was memorized but also all the other information they had in their brains that was related to that outline. The benefit was that people could now use information stored in their brain on a much more comprehensive level than before. The experience creates a kind of mental filing cabinet so that when you go to your brain to retrieve what you have memorized, you are also able to retrieve every other detail you know and understand connected to that memorized item. That experience convinced me of the power of the principle of reduction.

In another example, when I read a very important book—so important that I know I have to master its content—I underline the book as I read. Then, when I am finished, I will go back and type up all the underlined material, add the chapter titles and any subcategories that may be outlined in the book, include any transitional information that may be helpful in linking different underlined sections in the book, and in the end, I have an outline of the entire book. If there are good quotes, I include them as well. When finished, I have a very tight summary of the book, and when I want to review, I rarely go to the book. I go to the outline. I find the ratio about ten to one. That is, a 250-page book will reduce to an outline of about twenty-five pages. Through that process, I retain much more than if I merely read the whole book. That is another example in my experience of the power of reduction.

So, principle number one when teaching for memorization is to reduce the information to be memorized to its irreducible minimum. In some cases, as in medical school for example, that may still be a formidable amount of information, but nevertheless, you only memorize that which must be retained.

Preview

The learner must see the big picture of what he is to remember. The parts are more easily remembered when they are seen in relationship to the whole. Therefore, the teacher can show a graph, picture, or chart, tell a story, talk through an outline, or do something to help the learner see the big picture so that the learner knows where he is going ahead of time.

It is the principle of:

Step #1: Tell learners what you are going to tell them.

Step #2: Tell them.

Step #3: Tell them what you told them.

This may feel redundant to those who already know the information and are teaching, but to the typical learner, it is an important principle if we are to make sure the learner is following what is being taught. So, if you are teaching for memory, you must include a preview.

Activity

The learner must actively participate in the memorization process. For example, if the learner recites things out loud, fills in blanks, takes notes, draws maps, and recites things over and over, it will engage the learner's mind and increase memory. In our Walk Thru the Bible seminars, the participants memorized the outline of the Old Testament by also doing hand signs for each of the outline points. The first four points of the outline in the Old Testament were: Creation, Fall, Flood, Nations. And there was a hand sign for each of those points. The hand signs were powerful activity measures that were instrumental in people being able to recall so much information in a single day. So, if you are teaching for memory, you can include things that keep the learner active in the memorization process.

Progressivity

The learner memorizes more effectively if he learns one thing and then attaches the next new thing to it. For example, rather than trying to memorize an entire Scripture passage of five verses at once, the learner can memorize verse one. When he has that mastered, then he goes to the second verse. When the second one is memorized, he links one and two. Once he has one and two firmly memorized together, he then learns three and recites one, two, and three, and so on. This is sometimes called *chain-link learning*. If larger amounts of material are to be memorized, start with memorizing the first thing, and then attach the next thing to it. When those two things are mastered, attach the next thing to it, and so on. If you are teaching for memory, it is valuable to use progressivity or chain-link learning.

Creativity

If something is unusual, it sticks on the mind more effectively. So, if a teacher uses creativity when teaching for memory, it will help the student remember. For example, years ago when I was teaching home Bible studies, I would put down a book on the floor to represent the

Sea of Galilee, a necktie below it for the Jordan River, and two books, end to end, for the Dead Sea. I made a sofa the Mediterranean Sea, a golf ball was the Persian Gulf (golf), a little handmade palm tree was Kadesh-Barnea, and so on. Then, I took a G.I. Joe type of action character, dressed him up in a handkerchief to look like a little Israelite, and I moved him around the floor to the different geographical areas of the Old Testament to represent the movement of the Israelites as I told the Old Testament story. That type of creativity increases memory. *Sesame Street* is renowned for its creativity in teaching, which always helps increase memory. When you are teaching for memory, it is important to be creative.

Multiplicity

Memory is enhanced when more than one perceptual system is used. That is, if the person is taking in information through sight, hearing, and sense of touch, it triples his learning capacity. So, show him a map of Israel and talk through the locations, have him write in the names of cities on a map, and have him recite the names of the cities to a partner. This uses—in order—the sight gate (seeing the map), the muscle gate (writing), and the ear gate (hearing the names). If you are teaching for memory, the more perceptual systems used, the more effective the memorization.

Feedback

Memory is reinforced if the learner has immediate feedback on whether his learning attempts are right or wrong. So, if you are reciting a list of presidents out loud, and twenty-four other students say, "Lincoln," and you say, "Grant," you have immediate feedback. Or, you can take a quiz and grade it on the spot. Or recite to a partner and have the partner correct you if you make a mistake. With immediate feedback, mistakes are more easily erased and accuracy reinforced. When teaching for memory, give the learners immediate feedback.

Repetition

The more often a learner repeats a memory activity, the better he will remember it. That is why television and radio commercials often repeat a phone number three times—because studies have demonstrated that if most listeners hear a phone number three times, they will be able to remember it long enough to call it or write it down. The better the other memory methods are (preview, activity, creativity, etc.), the less repetition is required. Many people do not employ this method sufficiently, resulting in information that is only partially memorized or memorized for only a short period of time. But the reality is that memorizing something is like walking across a lawn. If you walk once, you cannot tell you ever walked across the lawn, but if you walk across it in the same place one hundred times, you wear a path.

The same is true in your brain. If the goal is to remember something for a long time, you need to review something often enough to wear a path in your brain.

Not only did we use these principles in Walk Thru the Bible Ministries, but I also used these principles when I wrote my first book, *30 Days to Understanding the Bible.* I wrote the list of methods to be used when teaching for memory on a 3-by-5-inch card and tacked it up on a bulletin board in front of me when I was writing *30 Days to Understanding the Bible.* That book has had a strong presence for over twenty years because by using these principles, people successfully memorize large amounts of information and then are able to retrieve, not only the memorized material from the book, but everything else they also know that is attached to the memorized information.

If we are not using these methods, we are not teaching for memory. We may think or hope we are, but we are not. So master this list and use it in your ministry when memory is to be gained.

Understanding: The Ability to Comprehend What Has Been Taught

When teaching for comprehension, the following are methods that are effective in contributing to that ministry goal:

▶ **Questions**

▶ **Restatement**

▶ **Summary**

Questions

Asking questions is the surest way to fill in the blanks of a subject that you do not understand. The most instinctive thing in the world to do when you do not understand something is to ask a question. So, the opportunity to ask and answer questions is a central part of any ministry where understanding is to be gained and should be used if you are teaching for understanding.

Restatement

State something in your own words. This is the surest way to be certain the learner comprehends something. If a learner cannot state something in his own words, the greatest likelihood is that he does not yet understand it. If a learner cannot state something in his own words, he is usually able to do so after asking a few questions. So, when trying to understand something yourself, or when you are teaching for understanding, require that something be restated in one's own words.

Summary

Summarize something you have learned. When you boil down a larger body of information to its irreducible minimum, it forces and creates a level of understanding that few other things do. And once the subject has been reduced, the mind tends to recall it better as well.

Another form of summarizing is to create a brief outline from a larger body of information. So again, when trying to understand something yourself, or when you are teaching for understanding, require that larger blocks of material be summarized.

Questions, restatement, and summary are three practical and immediately usable methods to employ if you are teaching for understanding. All of these methods require that you understand something in order to do it. The teacher or pastor or discipler who wants to encourage understanding will be careful to employ these methods. If you are not using these methods, you are not teaching for understanding. You may think or hope you are, but you are not. So master this list and use it in your ministry when memory is to be gained. I wrote this list on a 3-by-5-inch card and kept it in front of me when I was creator and general editor of the thirty-two-volume *Holman Bible Commentary* series. It was a powerful guide to me as I was putting together the methodology for the series as well as editing all thirty-two manuscripts that came in to me.

Application: The Ability to Recall Facts and Other Things You Have Learned and Apply Them in a New Situation in Your Own Life or Ministry

When teaching for application, effective methods include:

▶ **Personal Example**

▶ **Real Example**

▶ **Hypothetical Example**

Personal Example

Give an example of how the truth applies to your own life. Articulate how it will affect you if you apply the truth and how it will affect you if you do not. Or, you might have a real example of how the truth has already affected your life related to whether you did or did not respond properly to the truth. When teaching for application, encourage the recollection of personal examples that demonstrate what happens if you do or do not employ the truth being learned.

Real Example

Give an example of how the truth applies to another real situation not directly involving you. Again, you might recall how the truth impacted a situation involving others, or you might speculate on how it would have impacted them if they had or had not responded to the truth. This is one of the primary roles of storytelling or giving illustrations in teaching and preaching. When teaching for application, encourage the use of real examples to demonstrate what happens when one does or does not apply the truth being learned.

Hypothetical Example

Create a hypothetical example of something good that might happen if the truth is applied and something bad that might happen if the truth is violated. This is one powerful use for sermon stories, illustrations, and even jokes that are not true but make a strong point. When Jesus taught in parables, the parables were hypothetical examples, not real examples, of attitudes, values, and behavior that Jesus wanted His disciples to apply. When they did not understand the parables, they asked Him questions, and He answered them. When teaching for application, encourage the use of hypothetical examples to demonstrate what happens when one does or does not apply the truth being learned.

For example, if a person learns for the first time the verse, "*Like* a city that is broken into *and* without walls is a man who has no control over his spirit" (Prov. 25:28), he must then be helped to apply this truth to a new situation. Easiest is in his own life, though as the person matures and his ministry expands, he will be on the lookout for ways of applying it in other people's lives.

In applying it to himself, the learner must think of times when he has lost control of his spirit and what the negative consequences were. Then, having identified that personal weakness, he may be led to articulate how the loss of control damaged him or someone else and what the person might have done not to lose control—or what help might be necessary not to lose control again in the future.

These are not the only methods that can be employed for these educational goals. There are more methods that can be added to this basic list, and as you gain additional experience, you may add to them. However, time and experience have convinced me that this set of lists is concise enough, obvious enough, and usable enough to be of tremendous value to most teachers or disciplers.

This overview tells us, then, that when teaching, the teacher must know what his ministry goal is and must use methods appropriate to that goal. If you teach without using memory methods, do not be surprised if the learner does not remember what you have taught.

Conclusion

When I began my first year teaching in a Christian college, right out of seminary, I overwhelmed the students by dumping truckloads of information on them in a basic Bible doctrines class. Eager to impart as much information as I could in the time available, I hurtled through complex doctrinal information at a blinding speed. I can talk at about 250 words per minute, and most people can write at about 50 words per minute. It was a speedwriting class more than a basic theology class as students labored furiously to capture every word. Little mushroom clouds would rise from Bic pens as they spontaneously combusted.

Then one day, something life changing happened. I remember announcing the next major heading during a lecture: "The Derivation and Perpetuation of the Immaterial Part of Man," which I expected everyone to write down in preparation for what I would say next.

From the back of the large classroom, uttered at a barely audible level by a retired Air Force sergeant who was starting a second career as a pastor, came a slow and muffled, "The derivation and the what?!?" The class broke up laughing, and for the first time, I realized what I was doing. I tried to adjust on the fly and said, "Where the immaterial part of man came from and how it is passed along."

"Well, why didn't you just say so?!?" he muttered softly.

That experience rocked my world, and I decided I was not going to continue doing unto my students as had been done unto me for the twelve years of my higher education. The next year, I revamped everything. I had a certain body of information I wanted the class to memorize, another body of information I wanted them to understand, and a third body of information I wanted them to be able to apply.

If you teach without using memory methods, do not be surprised if the learner does not remember what you have taught.

I had them read and write papers outside of class on the information I wanted them to understand and apply, and we spent time in class memorizing the information I wanted them to remember. During the class, while I sometimes answered questions to further understanding, and occasionally spent time applying truth when especially relevant, I primarily used the methods for teaching when memory is the goal. I made ample use of the entire list of memory-enhancing methods for most of the period. The final exam was 170 fill-in-the-blank questions (for memory) involving the details of theology, definitions, central Scripture passages, and implications, along with two essays—one for understanding and one for application. The most common grade was one hundred. Nearly everyone got an A on the exam and an A in the class. Those who did not were the ones who did not show up for class and simply were not involved students.

Later, when the academic dean saw the grade report from that class, with the majority of students getting one hundred on the final and an A in the class—which did not fit the standard bell curve—he set an appointment to investigate. I explained carefully what I had done, and why, and showed him the final exam. He read it over carefully, looked up at me after several minutes, and said, "I'm not sure I would be able to get an A on this exam." He handed it back to me, said, "Carry on," and walked out of the room.

I was never the same.

I came to believe deeply that we have tremendous power to help change people if we will simply use the principles of how God has created us to learn.

A critical thing to understand is that, if we are hoping to create a ministry that encourages people to become complete Christians, there will be times when we will need to teach so that they remember some things. Other times, they will need to understand. Still other times, they will need to apply. We must become skilled in teaching for all three levels of knowledge.

In summary, God has created us to learn in a certain way. Educational research has identified how we learn and change, and Scripture has exemplified them. Therefore, our goals must be clear in three areas: what we want a disciple to know, be, and do. Also, our methodology must match our goals, and that methodology is not open to debate but has been handed to us through educational research and biblical example.

This reminds me of Hutch's classes... But this feels like its only helpful in a classroom setting...

Review for Memory

1. There are three ministry goals:
   a. K _nowledge_
   b. L _ifestyle_
   c. M _inistry_ S _kill_ (Page 127)

2. There are three subcategories of teaching for knowledge:
   a. M _emory_
   b. U _nderstanding_
   c. A _pplication_ (Page 126)

3. The eight methods of teaching for memory are:
   a. P _review_
   b. R _eduction_
   c. A _ctivity_
   d. P _rogressivity_
   e. C _reativity_
   f. M _ultiplicity_
   g. F _eedback_
   h. R _epetition_ (Page 127)

4. The three methods of teaching for understanding are:
   a. Q _uestions_
   b. R _estatement_
   c. S _ummary_ (Page 133)

5. The three methods of teaching for application are:
   a. P _ersonal_ Example
   b. R _eal_ Example
   c. H _ypothetical_ Example (Pages 134–35)

Review for Understanding

Write a one-sentence summary statement of each of the methods presented in a way that would be most valuable to you upon review. It may be a snippet from the existing paragraph. You may even want to change the word (i.e. preview = big picture), so that it is easier for you to remember:

Memory: *Recollection of knowledge*   Feedback: *Immediate awareness of whether they're right or wrong*

Preview: *Tell them what you will tell them   Tell them   Tell what you told them*   Repetition: *Doing something against again*

Activity: *Engagement in memorizing*   Understanding: *Comprehension of info.*

Progressivity: *Chain-link learning*   Questions: *Asking for clarification*

Creativity: *Teaching in an unusual way*   Restatement: *Phrasing something in your own words*

Multiplicity: *Use various senses to teach*   Summary: *Boiling info. down to the irreducible minimum*

Review for Application

How well did your educational experience match the methods for teaching for knowledge? What was done well? What was not done well? How will you change as a result?

It was all info download and repetition. Multiplicity and activity were not done well. I want learning to be creative and have long-term results!

CHAPTER 14

Central Passage: "Be imitators of God, as beloved children" (Eph. 5:1).

Lifestyle Methods Must Match Lifestyle Goals

To help a Christian master what he needs to be, lifestyle methods must be used.

Having identified the knowledge methods that must match knowledge goals in the previous chapter, we now turn our attention to lifestyle and skill methods. We saw earlier in the seven marks of a complete Christian that helping a Christian worship individually and corporately and helping a Christian impact the church and world are relatively easy compared to the central challenge of helping a Christian grow spiritually. Within that more difficult goal of spiritual growth, there are three subcomponents: growing in knowledge, growing in Christlike lifestyle, and growing in ministry skill.

The single greatest challenge of the Christian life is changing our attitudes, values, and behavior—our lifestyle—from who we are to who Jesus is.

Educational research tells us that if we want to influence a person's attitudes, values, and behavior, there are certain methods that must be used. When Christians hear that, they might wonder, *Well, does that mean that all I have to do is use the right methods, and another person will grow to maturity in Christ? What about the Bible? What about the Holy Spirit? Are they not the instruments of spiritual change in a Christian's life?*

Good questions.

And the answers are not simple. However, this is what seems to be true. If you use the education methods for influencing a person's attitudes, values, and behavior without the simultaneous involvement of the Bible, prayer, and Holy Spirit, a person will not become mature in Christ.

However, if you use the Bible and prayer, and the Holy Spirit is involved as the result of prayer and faith, you will have greater impact if you also use effective methods than if you do not. As we said earlier, you cannot violate the laws of teaching any more than you can violate the laws of nature.

Dr. Hendricks used to say to his seminary classes, "If you're going to bore people, bore them with physics or bore them with Shakespeare, but don't bore them with the Bible!" Good advice. And offered precisely because many of us have been bored to tears with the Bible. It is possible to teach the Bible in such a way as to drain the life out of it, to make it a fossilized collection of irrelevant or incomprehensible information with paralyzing results.

That is precisely why Solomon wrote:

> In addition to being a wise man, the Preacher also taught the people knowledge; and he pondered, searched out and arranged many proverbs. The Preacher sought to find delightful words and to write words of truth correctly. The words of wise men are like goads, and masters of *these* collections are like well-driven nails; they are given by one Shepherd. (Eccl. 12:9–11)

This passage tells us several things.

1. Solomon, a wise man, worked hard to distill the truth and to write the truth in the most effective way he could.

2. The reason he did that was in order to make a greater impact on the learner.

3. If the learner masters this well-compiled and well-articulated information, it will make a significant impact in his life.

It seems clear that all teachers and those in ministry should strive for the same goal—to make our material as interesting and relevant as possible, because in doing so, we make a greater impact in the lives of those we teach.

So, it seems reasonable to say, then, that **we cannot make the impact in others' lives without the strong involvement of the Bible, prayer, and the Holy Spirit, but even with the involvement of the Bible, prayer, and the Holy Spirit, we must also strive to obey the laws of teaching and learning that God has created**. We are no wiser to ignore these laws than to ignore the laws of gravity or aerodynamics. God uses both, and we pay the predictable price when we violate them.

Having said that, we return to the laws of teaching when we want to impact a person's attitudes, values, and behavior. There are discoverable laws of teaching for change in attitudes, values, and behavior.

Lifestyle Methods

Educational research tells us that the following are effective methods to use when our goal is to influence a person's attitudes, values, and behavior.

- ▶ **Modeling**
- ▶ **Examples**
- ▶ **Evaluation**
- ▶ **Exposure**
- ▶ **Instruction**
- ▶ **Challenge**

Modeling

Both the Bible and educational research teach us that life-on-life is the greatest methodology for affecting someone's attitudes, values, and behavior. In Mark 3:14, we read that Jesus appointed twelve disciples "so that they would be with Him." Proximity was crucial to Jesus' discipleship process. He wanted His disciples to be with Him. In John 1:35–39, two disciples of John the Baptist left John and followed Jesus. Jesus turned and asked them what they wanted. They said, "Rabbi (which translated means Teacher), where are You staying?" Jesus said, "Come, and you will see." So they followed Him and stayed with Him that day.

Jesus could have said, "My office is at the corner of Main Street and Elm. My hours are nine to five, Monday through Friday. Make an appointment, and I'll work you in." But He did not. He said, "Come and see."

The way God has created us, there is no more powerful influence in life than the presence of another life.

That is why parenting is the most powerful influence in the world. It is also why mentoring of kids and adults is such a powerful method. Lifestyle is more easily caught than taught.

The same is true in discipleship. We want people not just to know, understand, and mentally apply the Bible. We also want them to be deeply changed by it. So, we cannot be content only to instruct. Life-on-life modeling must be central to the process.

This brings up the power of integrity and moral authority. There is no more powerful influence you can have in the life of another person above being a person of integrity and high moral authority. The leader in any ministry sets a glass ceiling for most of those to whom he or she is ministering. Most people will not go beyond the level of spiritual maturity that you set. Therefore, if you want people to rain, you must cloudburst. If you want people to burn for the Word, you must combust.

146

Exposure

Exposure to others who model the attitudes, values, and behavior being taught is a second powerful way to influence attitudes, values, and behavior. This might be exposure to a famous individual, an exemplary individual who is not famous, or a group of people who model the attitudes, values, and behaviors being taught. A friend of mine was deeply impacted in his Christian life by a chance and brief encounter with Billy Graham. I have been deeply impacted by any number of people who were godly examples for the Christian life but were not the least bit famous.

Finally, there is the power of the group. I became a Christian after my first year in college at a state university. As a result of becoming a Christian, I transferred to a Christian liberal arts college. Not having grown up in an overtly Christian home and having had plenty of time to learn non-Christian behavior in my first year in college, it was a profound learning experience for me to be immersed in a campus of Christians. The power of the group was life changing for me as I learned a great deal about living the Christian life simply by observing those around me.

As we disciple, we must be alert to the transforming influence of others who model the attitudes, values, and behavior being taught, whether they be famous individuals, non-famous individuals, or a group.

Examples

Another powerful influence for attitudes, values, and behavior are examples—both real and fictional—from history, literature, and movies, who exemplify the attitudes, values, and behavior being taught. Reading about, hearing about, or seeing movies about exemplary people, real or fictional, can be a great source of inspiration for living an exemplary authentic Christian life. Corrie ten Boom,

Brother Andrew, Chuck Colson, William Wilberforce, and other great Christians of past generations can be soul-stirring examples to us.

Non-Christians who exhibit remarkable Christian traits can also be powerful influences. Winston Churchill's speech in which he admonished us to "never give up," has been a repeated source of inspiration for me. The classic fiction *Robinson Crusoe*[1] was a deep inspiration to me, as well, even though Robinson Crusoe was not even real. I will never forget reading, "God will often deliver us in a manner that seems, initially, to destroy us." I was changed forever just by reading that one line. Finally, I was also deeply moved by the example of Judah in the movie *Ben Hur*, as he turned his back on the world in order to pursue Christ.

If we are Christians trying to make progress ourselves, we can deliberately expose ourselves to good examples both real and fictional. If we are teaching or discipling, we can draw on these same examples as part of our ministry to others.

Instruction

We can also draw on the teaching of exemplary, authoritative sources. For example, when we are teaching ways that a husband can more effectively express his love for his wife, we can draw on the teachings of James Dobson who has interviewed and polled thousands of women to discover what their deepest felt needs were and how their husbands could meet them.[2] His training, his experience, and his extraordinary insight all make him a powerful, authoritative figure in the field of Christian marriage. Therefore, when we draw on the teachings of authoritative figures like him, we increase our influence on those to whom we minister.

Similar examples could be given in the area of finances, being effective in the workplace as a Christian, being an effective parent, and so on. When we are ministering in these areas, we can draw on strong authoritative sources to give added influence to our ministry.

Of course, the Bible is the ultimate authoritative source. So, though it may seem obvious, we conclude by saying that we can draw on no higher authoritative source than teaching the Bible as we seek to positively influence the attitudes, values, and behavior of the people to whom we are ministering. Effectively teaching the Bible is a powerful force for life change, not only because of the power of the Word, but also because the Holy Spirit illumines our minds to the truth of Scripture and applies it to our lives.

Evaluation

When trying to influence the lifestyle of another individual, it is helpful to provide self-evaluation to illuminate potential needed change. Even though a Christian might be exposed to all the right people and information to lead him to positive change, it is still possible for much of the truth to go zinging high over his head unless he is brought to a moment of self-evaluation.

For example, after teaching on the need for Christians to be honest and ethical, we might present a difficult situation and then ask the learner, "What would you do in this situation?" Or we might ask, "Have you ever been in a similar situation in which you failed to do the right thing?"

Effectively teaching the Bible is a powerful force for life change . . .

Or in another example, we might give the learner a temperament or personality test. These tests typically list the strengths and weaknesses of certain temperament or personality profiles. We then might ask the learner to compile a list of actual personal weaknesses out of the potential weaknesses suggested in the profile report. We might ask the learner to find Scripture passages that speak to each of those weaknesses and to begin a process of Scripture memorization and meditation as a way to begin making progress on those weaknesses. I know I have done just that—with great profit. Introducing the self-evaluation process to the learning experiences encourages life change.

Challenge

Sometimes, we know the truth, and we are simply not doing it. In those cases, it might be valuable for us to be challenged to change. Before I became a Christian, I used to swear like a drunken sailor. After I became a Christian, my language cleaned up dramatically. However, there were still times when I gave myself the freedom to use the stronger versions of *heck* and *darn*. Then someone lovingly, but unambiguously, challenged me that such language was not appropriate for a Christian. I thought about it, concluded she was right, and quit using that language.

We have to use discernment when challenging people. Not everyone is the same. Some people only need a gentle word of direction as I did, while other people might need a proverbial swift kick in the pants. I have had people tell me that it is not helpful when people are subtle. They do not get subtlety. They confessed to needing and wanting the swift kick. However, it must be used with great caution. Often, what is appropriate is something between gentle direction and a swift kick. We may be able to effectively work the method of challenge into a nonconfrontational component of a lesson plan or ministry session.

These are certainly not the only methods that can be used when we are attempting to influence the attitudes, values, and behavior of individuals. There are many more variations of possible examples that could be given for each point. The goal here is not to give a technical and exhaustive list of available methods but rather to give a strong sample of the kinds of things that are effective to guide us and to whet our appetites for more. Experience and creativity will expand these possibilities significantly.

Review for Memory

1. We cannot make a spiritual impact in others' lives without the strong involvement of the B_idole_____ and the H_oly_____ S_pirit_____. (Page 143)

2. Even with the involvement of the Bible and the Holy Spirit, we must also strive to obey the laws of t_eaching_____ and l_earning_____ that God has created. (Page 143)

3. There are six steps in teaching to change attitudes, values, and behavior:
   a. M_odeling_____
   b. E_xposure_____
   c. E_xamples_____
   d. I_nstruction_____
   e. E_valuation_____
   f. C_hallenge_____ (Page 143)

Review for Understanding

Write a one-sentence summary statement of each of the lifestyle methods in a way that would be most valuable to you upon review. You may use a snippet from the existing paragraph in the text or use your own words:

Modeling: _Life-on-life_

Exposure: _Transforming influence of others who model the attitudes, values, & behavior being taught_

Examples: _People who exemplify what is taught_

Instruction: _Exemplary, authoritative sources_

Evaluation: _self-evaluation_

Challenge: _Feedback_

Review for Application

Give an example of when you were impacted in your lifestyle by an experience. Which method(s) do you remember the most vividly?

Feedback on the World Race... This was invaluable because it aided my growth process by helping me to recognize my blind spots and also encourage me in my strengths.

CHAPTER 15

Central Passage: *"Be imitators of me, just as I also am of Christ" (1 Cor. 11:1).*

Ministry Skill Methods Must Match Ministry Skill Goals

To help a Christian master what he needs to do, ministry skill methods must be used.

Almost anything is difficult to do well. Something as simple as using a yo-yo is difficult to do well and requires training. Something as complicated as learning to play the piano well takes an amazing amount of time. The same is true of ministry skills. Each Christian is given two jobs—both of which require training. The first job is sharing his faith. The second job is using his spiritual gifts. Both can be done without training, but both go better with training.

The church must use effective training techniques to teach believers how to teach, how to share their faith, how to counsel others, and how to disciple. **We do it the way Jesus did it in Scripture, and we do it the way educational research confirms is effective: we demonstrate the entire skill, we break the skill down to its parts and demonstrate the parts, we practice the skill with supervision, and finally, we master the skill through repetition under realistic conditions.**

▶ Demonstrate

▶ Divide

▶ Practice

▶ Master

Demonstrate

The first step in acquiring skill is to see the skill demonstrated in its entirety. Whether it is something relatively simple like learning to putt the golf ball or something more complex like learning how to teach a lesson, it is still most effective to see the skill demonstrated in its entirety. That way, the learner knows the whole of what he is trying to learn.

Divide

The second step in acquiring a skill is to see the skill broken down into its component parts and to observe a step-by-step demonstration of each part. This allows the learner to focus on each of the steps in the process and make sure that he did not overlook something when he saw the overall demonstration. It is important to have each step explained as it is demonstrated.

Practice

The third step is for the learner to practice each component part under supervision to make sure that he is practicing correctly. If a mistake is made, it can be corrected, and another attempt can be made to get it right. If the learner discovers right away that he has done something correctly, it is more likely that he will do it correctly again. It is helpful for the learner to get less and less guidance during this step as his skill increases. Then the learner acquires habits that he is able to repeat in the future.

Master

The learner then continues to practice under realistic conditions until mastery is gained. Even though a learner may know exactly how to do something and may rehearse the individual steps accurately, it still may take vast repetition in order to gain mastery.

I once attempted to learn how to juggle. The individual teaching me followed these four steps. He juggled while I watched. Then he demonstrated the component parts of juggling. Third, he had me practice each of the steps while he watched so that he could make comments and help me do each step correctly. Lastly, I had to practice under realistic conditions until mastery was gained. By realistic conditions I mean that I had to use little juggling pouches. I could not just imagine juggling or have a picture of someone juggling. I had to use juggling pouches and attempt to juggle. I was an utter failure, not because I had not seen a demonstration that time, not because I had not seen a step-by-step demonstration of the whole process, and not because I had not practiced under supervision. I failed because I was not willing to invest the time needed to practice until mastery was gained. It was harder than I thought it would be. But that is the process nevertheless.

By contrast, one of the most complex and difficult tasks ever performed by a human being is the flying of a fighter jet. The process is so complex mentally and so demanding physically that only a small fraction of humanity is capable of doing it. Vast amounts of information have to be mentally processed almost instantaneously. In addition, the execution of highly sophisticated skills that are life-and-death in nature must be done perfectly and instantaneously. When the plane goes into a spin or stall, overcorrecting the joystick by as little as an inch can cause a pilot to lose complete control of the plane.

> I failed because I was not willing to invest the time needed to practice until mastery was gained.

Several years ago, I reviewed these four steps and asked an acquaintance who flew F-16 fighter jets if this was the way he learned how to fly his plane. After mulling it over for a few seconds, he said, "Yes." I asked the same question of a friend who flew helicopters in the Vietnam War, and his answer was the same. And notably, practicing under realistic conditions involved being both in a simulator and aircraft. So whether we are learning how to juggle or learning how to fly a sophisticated aircraft, these are the four steps that must be followed.

Of course, learning how to master an interpersonal skill such as teaching, counseling, or sharing one's faith is different than a purely physical skill, but the principles apply, nevertheless. This is exactly how I learned to preach in seminary.

In summary, God created us so that we learn how to master skills a certain way. Educational research has identified the steps in learning a skill. Therefore, if we are training a person to acquire a skill, we can have confidence by following these four steps.

Review for Memory

1. There are four steps in learning a skill:
   a. D_emonstrate_
   b. D_ivide_
   c. P_ractice_
   d. M_aster_____ (Page 151)

Review for Understanding

Write a one-sentence summary statement of each of the skill methods in a way that would be most valuable to you upon review. You may use a snippet from the existing paragraph in the text or use your own words:

Demonstrate: _Skill shown in its entirety_

Divide: _step-by-step demonstration_

Practice: _Practice each step under supervision_

Master: _Practicing in realistic circumstances_

Review for Application

Give an example of when you learned a skill. Articulate the component parts of the skill. Articulate how you think you could duplicate that experience in the life of someone you were ministering to.

Worship leading... ← Then in music memorization, rehearsals, stage presence, heart posture to God, sensitivity to the Spirit...

CHAPTER 16

Central Passage: *"And do not be conformed to this world, but be transformed by the renewing of your mind, so that you may prove what the will of God is, that which is good and acceptable and perfect" (Rom. 12:2).*

Capitalizing on How the Mind Works

The core issue in experiencing lifestyle change is mental renewal.

An increasing emphasis is being placed these days on the mental side of athletic performance. It is common for professional athletes, particularly professional golfers, to have mental coaches. Michael Jordan, one of the greatest basketball players ever, readily admitted that what set him apart was his mental tenacity.[1] Olympic champions know how to train their minds like they train their bodies. Using mental exercises they learn how to tune out distractions, focus on essentials, reduce stress, and increase concentration.

Gymnastic gold medalist Shannon Miller said, "The physical aspect of the sport will only take you so far. The mental aspect has to kick in. What separates the gold medalists from the silver medalists is simply the mental game."[2]

Athletes commonly practice five disciplines:[3]

1. Visualize the desired outcome. Using mental imagery, athletes can envision peak performance in exacting detail and, in doing so, lift their physical performance to the level of their mental

visualization. The brain does not distinguish between a real and a vividly imagined event. Therefore, mental rehearsal is almost as effective as physical training in many instances. Capitalizing on this phenomenon, athletes can continue to train even when they are resting their bodies to keep from overtraining physically.

2. Meditate daily. Many athletes draw on traditional meditation practices, listening to calming music, chanting mantras, lighting candles and incense, and trying to make the mind go blank. In this way they can reduce stress and restore a sense of calm.

3. Reject negative thinking. Using instructional and motivational self-talk, athletes clear their minds of negative and self-sabotaging thoughts and learn to affirm positive thinking.

4. Set clear goals. The higher an athlete sets his goals, the harder he is motivated to work. Athletes often post their goals around the house so that they see them over and over throughout the day, ingraining the goals in their everyday thoughts.

5. Learn to concentrate. Athletes learn to develop their powers of concentration until they can focus clearly on the activity at hand and perform at a high level without a lot of conscious thought.

There are other disciplines that some athletes observe, but these are typical kinds of mental exercises that many top athletes engage in because the level of success is often determined by mental discipline and creativity.

Just as athletes can use the power of the mind for extraordinary physical achievement, so Christians can use the mind for extraordinary spiritual achievement. Matthew 22:37 says, "YOU SHALL LOVE THE LORD YOUR GOD WITH ALL YOUR HEART, AND WITH ALL YOUR SOUL, AND WITH ALL YOUR MIND." There could be many ways that we would love God with our mind, but one way is to discipline our minds, like spiritual athletes, to achieve an increased capacity to know, love, and serve God. If a Christian were to accept—not metaphorically, but in reality—the challenge to become a spiritual Olympian, it would lay out for him a course of action that would make the normal Christian life seem subnormal. If Christians were willing to pay the price to excel in a life of faith that many athletes are willing to pay for to excel in athletics, it would revolutionize how many of us live.

This is the challenge that Paul lays out to us in 1 Corinthians 9:24–27:

> Do you not know that those who run in a race all run, but *only* one receives the prize? Run in such a way that you may win. Everyone who competes in the games exercises self-control in all things. They then *do it* to receive a perishable wreath, but we an imperishable. Therefore I run in such a way, as not without aim; I box in such a way, as not beating the air; but I discipline my body and make it my slave, so that, after I have preached to others, I myself will not be disqualified.

Understanding How the Brain Works

I have personally been challenged by a greater understanding about how the brain works. We used to think that the brain was a physiologically static organ. That is, it was poured in concrete at birth and could not change in adulthood. That idea was turned on its head in the 1980s and 1990s when science made dramatic strides in technology including magnetic resonance imaging (MRI), positron emission tomography (PET), single photon emission computed tomography (SPECT), and magnetoencephalography (MEG). These new technologies allow scientists to peer deeply into the brain to see and to conclude things that have altered forever our understanding of this magnificent organ. This glimpse into the remarkable things we are learning about the brain has left us shaking our heads in wonder. We are now able to map the brain's electrical activity in detail and are able to actually watch the brain think in real time.[4]

By getting a closer look at the functioning of the various parts of the brain, we have a greater understanding of which part of the brain controls which mental functions. This has led to an increased understanding of the basic divisions of the brain: the conscious brain and the non-conscious brain. The non-conscious brain is something like a million times more powerful than the conscious brain. The conscious brain operates with a very short-term memory span, generally limited to twenty seconds or less. The non-conscious brain remembers everything it experiences forever.

The non-conscious brain is responsible for the majority of our thinking. "We are aware of a tiny fraction of the thinking that goes on in our minds, and we can control only a tiny part of our conscious thoughts. The vast majority of our thinking efforts goes on subconsciously." [5]

Often, our subconscious attitudes, values, and behaviors are at odds with our conscious attitudes, values, and behavior.

"We're finding that we have these unconscious behavioral guidance systems that are continually furnishing suggestions through the day about what to do next, and the brain is considering and often acting on those, all before conscious awareness. Sometimes those goals are in line with our conscious intentions and purposes, and sometimes they're not." [6]

Because of this, there is great significance to the Christian in understanding the role and power of the subconscious mind in spiritual behavior. Often, our subconscious attitudes, values, and behavior are at odds with our conscious attitudes, values, and behavior. For example, as we observed in chapter 2, in our conscious mind we may know the verse that says, "My God will supply all your needs according to His riches in glory in Christ Jesus" (Phil. 4:19). And we may think we believe that and that we are trusting God. But in our subconscious mind, we may not be so sure. We may subconsciously question God's readiness to meet our needs. Or we may be concerned that God might not supply all our needs to the degree to which we have become accustomed. That is, we might have food and clothing—which classify as the barest human needs according to 1 Timothy 6:8, "If we have food and covering, with these we shall be content"—but face homelessness, a situation that would terrify most Americans. As a result, when our financial security is threatened, we respond in fear rather than peace, with the fear coming from our subconscious thoughts and values.

Therefore, one of the great challenges for the Christian is to bring the attitudes, values, and behavior of the conscious mind in harmony with the attitudes, values, and behavior of the non-conscious mind.

One of the major ways to drive conscious thoughts into the non-conscious mind is through repetition.

Scientists are now using the word *neuroplasticity* to describe the capacity of the brain to change in ways we never imagined. If we exercise our brains properly, we can change our brains, taking them to new heights of mental achievement, in the same way that we exercise our bodies to take them to new heights of physical achievement. Scientists call this *neural reconditioning*. Neuroscientists have an expression: "Neurons that fire together wire together."[7] **This means that as a new thought pattern is repeated over and over, the neural patterns in your brain literally wire themselves together, building a brand-new network of neurons, creating a superhighway in the brain, enabling us to change in more and greater ways.**[8]

As an example of this, when I was young, I watched a documentary wherein NASA outfitted astronauts-in-training with goggles with special lenses that turned their vision upside down when they wore them. As they pushed the boundaries of human limitations for the sake of the space program, the scientists wanted to see how the body would react to such an extreme alteration in visual perception. This, of course, presented profound challenges to the astronauts in performing even the most basic functions of life. Every movement appeared opposite of reality, causing them to internally have to think through each motion, rather than just reacting instinctively, based on what they saw. However, approximately thirty days later, an amazing thing happened. Their world turned right side up again. Their brains found a way to rewire themselves so that now, even with the goggles on, they were able to see everything right side up.

It seems that it takes about thirty days of consistently applying reconditioning techniques for our non-conscious brain to rewire itself and give us a new capacity to view life. This is profound for the Christian because it suggests that if we are diligent in using our conscious brain to impact our non-conscious brain, we can begin to change in important ways in as little as thirty days.

The way we use the conscious brain to impact our non-conscious brain, as we have seen, is to repeat thought patterns over and over again, causing neural patterns in the brain to rewire themselves, building a brand new network of neurons, creating a superhighway in the brain, enabling us to change in more and greater ways. This suggests that as we memorize Scripture and meditate on its truth over and over again, the brain will rewire itself, enabling us to conform to its truth as the process drives the truth from our conscious to non-conscious mind.

Gary Smalley gives testimony to this process in his book *Change Your Heart, Change Your Life.* He said that serious stress in his life caused a heart attack and kidney failure. For the third time in his life, he surrendered his life to God. He had no options. He was literally killing himself with stress. So he selected Scripture passages that spoke to his immediate situation, studied them to learn the full meaning of them, memorized them deeply, and thought about them over and over every day.

Smalley said that it took him several weeks of memorizing and rehearsing Scripture over and over again until his fundamental reaction to life's trials changed. The stress dissolved, his perspective improved, and he gained a whole new ability to deal with the unpleasantries of life. He learned that if we surrender all expectations to God and trust Him with the results, it takes stress off.[9] Once this principle lodges in our hearts, it can give us a virtually stress-free life. Memorizing and meditating on Scripture are the keys to having this principle lodge deeply in our hearts.

Smalley's experience is consistent with scientific observations about neuroplasticity. By thinking a thought over and over again, it wears a path in the brain. As this repetition is continued, the new path becomes a superhighway in the brain, enabling us to change in more and greater ways.

I read Smalley's book in a time of intense personal stress. In the providence of God, circumstances had conspired, from my limited human point of view at the time, to threaten my financial security, my health, and my ability to continue to minister. The stress was so severe that I began to experience ominous physical problems.

Staring into that circumstantial abyss, I came across his book and read it in twenty-four hours. I accepted his challenge to find Scripture verses that spoke to my intimidating circumstances, memorize them deeply, and begin to meditate on them many times every day. After five weeks, the stress dissipated. Nothing else changed. None of my intimidating circumstances improved. But I improved. The truth of the Scriptures rooted deeply into my mind, made its way into my subconscious, and began to affect, in a very positive way, my attitudes, values, and behavior.

My approach toward Scripture up to that point had been quantity over quality. That is, I had many verses memorized shallowly, a mile wide and an inch deep. So I changed and took the inch-wide and a

> [Smalley] learned that if we surrender all expectations to God and trust Him with the results, it takes stress off.

mile-deep approach. I took just a few Scripture passages, memorized them so deeply that you could shake me awake at three o'clock in the morning, and I could immediately recite them. Then I meditated on them over and over every day. This made a life-altering difference for me. The knot in my stomach dissolved, my preoccupation with negative consequences evaporated, and I began walking up out of the valley.

Smalley stated that he knew (in his conscious mind) the verses that should have solved his problems. But they did not. The reason is that he did not know them well enough and had not meditated on them deeply enough for their truth to seep into the subconscious mind, which is where they change attitudes, values, and behavior.[10] The same happened with me. In the example I gave earlier, I knew "My God will supply all your needs according to His riches in glory in Christ Jesus" (Phil. 4:19). But it did not help. Only after I memorized the passage deeply and spent five weeks meditating on it and other passages that spoke to my circumstances did the truth begin to change my fundamental responses to life.

It was only after that experience that I began to learn about the brain and neuroplasticity and neural reconditioning. It was only after that experience that I learned that neuroscientists would say, "Oh, of course. You took a new thought and rehearsed it over and over and over again so that the brain eventually rewired itself, giving you a new perspective."

That experience became a very powerful reinforcement to my belief in the value and power of scriptural memorization and meditation. And it intensified my convictions about guarding the mind to have a scientific explanation as to why.

Sincere and enlightened Christians want to be like Christ. It is His character and lifestyle to which we aspire. There are two passages of Scripture that help identify what that means in practical terms—in terms of character and lifestyle. First is Galatians 5:22–23, listing the fruit, or character qualities of the Holy Spirit: "The fruit of the Spirit is love, joy, peace, patience, kindness, goodness, faithfulness, gentleness, self-control." These are the personal traits to which we aspire as Christians, and why not? If we had peace, love, and joy, what else would we possibly want?

Second is 1 Corinthians 13:4–8, which defines the characteristics of love, which are important because 1 John 4:16 tells us that God is love, while Matthew 22:37–39 tells us that our two greatest responsibilities are to love God and love our neighbor:

> Love is patient, love is kind *and* is not jealous; love does not brag *and* is not arrogant, does not act unbecomingly; it does not seek its own, is not provoked, does not take into account a wrong *suffered*, does not rejoice in unrighteousness, but rejoices with the truth; bears all things, believes all things, hopes all things, endures all things. Love never fails. (1 Cor. 13:4–8)

So, if we are to become like Christ by taking on the fruit of the Spirit and manifesting the character qualities of love, it requires that we do two things. First, we must memorize and meditate on those passages over and over again. In addition, we must be very cautious about letting things into our minds that take us a different direction from those life qualities. Otherwise, poor stewardship of our minds will offset and neutralize the work we do in Scripture memorization and meditation.

Guarding the Mind

First, we must guard what we allow into our minds. When we allow a stream of things into our minds that take us away from our goal to be like Christ, it pollutes our integrity and retards our progress toward Christlikeness.

Second, we must guard what we allow our minds to create. Not all sinful and harmful influence comes from the outside. Our minds can create sinful and unhelpful thoughts, and we must guard against that.

Third, we must guard what we allow our minds to dwell on. Whether a wrong thought comes from the outside or whether we create it ourselves, we must guard against dwelling on these things. All because, as we think thoughts, they wear a path in the brain, and the more we think of a thought, the more deeply that path is worn, so that our brains become hardwired to facilitate that kind of thinking.

Then, after we have guarded our minds to suppress harmful and sinful things, we must encourage the input and creation of good things, helpful things, and godly things. In suppressing bad mental activity and encouraging good mental activity, we conform to the way God created us and the way He intends us to make positive spiritual progress. We hardwire our minds to facilitate biblical attitudes, values, and behavior.

Now when I read Psalm 1:1–3, I marvel at how we are "fearfully and wonderfully made" (139:14). I understand more specifically, in scientific terms, how the process of diligent biblical meditation creates a pattern of spiritual success in life.

> How blessed is the man who does not walk in the counsel
> of the wicked,
> Nor stand in the path of sinners,
> Nor sit in the seat of scoffers!
> But his delight is in the law of the LORD,
> And in His law he meditates day and night.
> He will be like a tree *firmly* planted by streams of water,
> Which yields its fruit in its season
> And its leaf does not wither;
> And in whatever he does, he prospers. (1:1–3)

Now when I read Philippians 4:8, I understand more specifically the power of keeping our thoughts only positive: "Finally, brethren, whatever is true, whatever is honorable, whatever is right, whatever is pure, whatever is lovely, whatever is of good repute, if there is any excellence and if anything worthy of praise, dwell on these things."

Now when I read Matthew 5:27–28, I understand more specifically the urgency of not allowing our minds to think on sinful things: "You have heard that it was said, 'YOU SHALL NOT COMMIT ADULTERY'; but I say to you that everyone who looks at a woman with lust for her has already committed adultery with her in his heart."

When we violate these verses, it creates pathways in our brain that lead us into sinful, harmful, and self-destructive attitudes, values, and behavior. When we conform to these verses, it creates pathways in our brains that lead us into righteous, helpful, and constructive attitudes, values, and behavior.

We ought to take the Scriptures at face value and obey their truth. And on one level I did. But learning about how the brain works strengthened, deepened, and intensified my belief and my convictions about it. It took me to another level of readiness to do all that the Scriptures teach.

In the language of the New Testament, there is a word for knowledge: *gnosko*. Then, there is another word for knowledge: *epignosko*, which is the same word, but intensified. It means not only to know, but to know exactly or thoroughly—to really know. An understanding of how the brain works has taken me from *gnosko* to *epignosko* regarding my convictions toward guarding the mind to suppress the bad and encourage the good.

Toward that end, I have collected a set of verses that I call Super-Verses. Just as there are some foods that pack extraordinary nutritional wallop, called super foods, so there are passages of Scripture that pack extraordinary spiritual wallop, and I call them SuperVerses. They are verses that speak directly to issues in my life in which I want to see improvement. I have memorized them deeply and mentally rehearse them daily and have done so for years. It has made a life-changing difference.

Not only have I made a significant investment in memorizing and meditating on Scripture, I have also compiled a list of biblical principles and affirmations that I review daily. Beyond that, and as a result of that, I have become much more judicious about what I allow into my mind and what I allow my mind to dwell on. This applies particularly to electronic media. The cumulative consequence of these disciplines has been exponential personal and spiritual progress. At an age when many are sliding into home, I feel that I am entering my prime. As I write this book, I am no longer a young man, but the last several years have been, by far, the most significant season of spiritual growth in my life, and I believe the best is yet to come.

> . . . I have become much more judicious about what I allow into my mind and what I allow my mind to dwell on.

I bring this subject up in this late chapter in the book to make a crucial point. As we craft a discipleship strategy for those to whom we are ministering, as we learn how to structure a ministry that identifies what we want our people to know, be, and do, and as we target these ministry goals with methods designed to more effectively further those goals, we must keep this perspective: **what people put into their minds, what they keep out of their minds, and what they allow their minds to create and to dwell on will determine who they become.** If they do this effectively, they will become spiritually mature and enjoy the fruit of love, joy, and peace. If they do this ineffectively, they will remain spiritually stunted and encumbered with trouble, frustration, and defeat.

So, throughout our discipleship process, we must continuously be aware of this and always be guiding and encouraging ourselves and our students to steward the use of our minds. If they do not see the importance of this naturally, it may help them (as it did me) to understand how the brain works. We become what we behold, as was said in chapter 2. Therefore, we must behold those things that get us where we want to go. For many of us, it will require that we either change our goals or change our behavior, because often our present behavior will not get us to our desired goals.

Championing Spiritual Growth

Practically, this means we champion the growth part of discipleship. We encourage careful stewardship of the mind, we encourage deep memorization, we encourage concentrated meditation, and we celebrate lofty spiritual goals. It means that we take the process seriously. People's lives and welfare are hanging in the balance.

Many people are lukewarm in the pursuit of their Christian life because the efforts they have expended in the past have not yielded the results they hoped for. I know that was the case with me for many years. The problem, of course, is not with the Christian life. The problem is with the efforts people have expended. If they are like me, they have not expended great enough effort in the direction of the right pursuits. I spent hours memorizing a hundred verses fairly well. I should have memorized fewer verses and spent more time meditating on them. And I should have been more careful about what I allowed into my mind.

I had devotions each day only to have the benefit neutralized by the natural effects of living in a fallen world. The ten minutes a day I spent in daily devotions were simply not adequate to offset the effect of the world in which we live. The unavoidable negative input that comes to us in the normal living of everyday life will rapidly overwhelm half-hearted measures to nurture our inner lives.

So, in our personal spiritual growth, and in our discipleship ministry, we must take into account how the brain works. The brain works by repetition and reinforcement. Our attitudes, values, and behavior are formed by that which we think about. If we are not serious students of Scripture, if we do not have regular personal worship time, and if we do not spend sufficient time nurturing our inner world, then our attitudes, values, and behavior become inexorably shaped by the attitudes, values, and behavior of the people around us. Television, music, movies, social media and the Internet, advertising, news broadcasts, and the hundred other influences in our everyday world will—by sheer repetition—take us the opposite direction of our conscious spiritual goals.

As disciplers, we must engage our students in a lifestyle of spiritual input that is sufficient to offset the influences that exist in the inescapable world around us. We must capitalize on how the brain works. And if we accept the challenge to discipline our minds for spiritual pursuits to the degree that top athletes discipline their minds for athletic pursuits, we will enter into quality of spiritual life that we will not, and cannot, know any other way.

Review for Memory

1. Just as athletes can use the power of the mind for extraordinary p _physical_ achievement, so Christians can use the mind for extraordinary s _piritual_ achievement. (Page 158)

2. Scientists are now using the word _neuroplasticity_ to describe the capacity of the brain to change in ways we never imagined in the past. (Page 161)

3. As a new thought pattern is repeated over and over, the neural patterns in your brain literally wire themselves together, building a brand-new network of neurons, creating a s _uperhighway_ in the brain, enabling us to c _hange_ in more and greater ways. (Page 161)

4. We must guard our minds in three ways:

a. We must guard what we a _llow_ into our minds.

b. We must guard what we allow our minds to c _reate_

c. We must guard what we allow our minds to d _well_ on. (Page 165)

5. As we disciple, we must take into account that what people p_ut_ i_nto_ their minds, what they k_eep_ o_ut_ of their minds, what they allow their minds to create and to d _well_ o_n_ will determine who they b_ecome_. (Page 168)

Review for Understanding

Summarize this chapter in one hundred words or fewer:

Repeated thoughts forge superhighways in the brain. We can take advantage of this reality by feeding our brains thoughts that will merge our conscious & subconscious so that we deeply know Scripture.

Review for Application

How effectively do you think you are using the power of your mind to grow spiritually? What do you think you need to change to begin using it more effectively?

NOT. I have been convicted about this for a while now. I need to deeply meditate on a verse to wear a new superhighway in my brain.

Central Passage: *"Everyone, after he has been fully trained, will be like his teacher" (Luke 6:40).*

Leading the Way

Disciplers set the spiritual
high-water mark for those
they disciple.

We started this book by saying that the Brave New World of the twenty-first century requires the rethinking of a Brave New Discipleship strategy. So let us review what is new about the discipleship strategy I am proposing in this book that will make it more effective in the twenty-first century. *Finally*

Leading the Way Professionally

As we consider how to be leaders in the task of discipling the next generation's leaders, we must lead the way professionally, and we must lead the way personally. In leading the way professionally, we must embrace a discipleship system that is deep, wide, and high.

Deep: Discipleship Strategy Must Have an Adequate Foundation

I watched the forty-seven-story AT&T building go up in midtown Atlanta. I was ministering with Walk Thru the Bible Ministries at the time, and our headquarters were right across the street from the building. They spent nearly a year working just on the foundation. Then, after only another year, they erected the entire forty-seven stories. I remember thinking as I watched the preparation work on the foundation, *At that rate they were never going to finish that building. If it took an entire year just for the foundation, how long would it take to build the rest of it?* The answer turned out to be not very long. It became a life parable to me of the importance of laying an adequate foundation for anything you want to build. The higher you want the building to be, the deeper you must build the foundation. And while it seems almost too obvious to say, if you have a small foundation, you can never build a great building. You cannot build a small foundation and then hope to erect a great building on it. It does not work that way.

The parallel to the Christian life is clear. The greater we want our Christian life to be, the more time must be spent on the foundation. That means we must identify the foundation of the irreducible minimum of knowledge, the fundamental marks of character, and the non-optional ministry abilities, and we cannot rest until we have inculcated those things into the willing heart.

Dr. Hendricks, former professor of Christian education at Dallas Theological Seminary, was fond of saying, "Most learning is self generated. So teach the basics, and teach them well." It rang true when I heard him say it many years ago, and the years that have passed have only confirmed the truth of it. If a Christian possesses a complete foundation for the Christian life, then with the leading and grace of God, he can build a towering Christian experience on it. But my own experience, as well as my observation, has been that if the foundation is not adequate, the superstructure will never be towering.

Someone might say, "That isn't unique to a new discipleship strategy. We have understood all along that an adequate foundation must be laid for the Christian life." And to that, I would agree. We have understood it. But in my experience and observation, even though we have understood it, we have not done a very good job of doing it.

> The greater we want our Christian life to be, the more time must be spent on the foundation.

I became a Christian after a very rowdy year at a state university where I majored in rock 'n' roll at night (I was a drummer in a rock band) and minored in euchre during the day (a popular card game in the student union). When I became a Christian that following summer, I had a significant backlog of attitudes, values, and behavior that were decidedly unchristian and had a lot of kinks that had to be worked out in my life as I started to grow spiritually. In pursuit of new spiritual values, I transferred to a Christian college, then went to a theological seminary, all the while going to church twice on Sundays and once in the middle of the week. I studied considerably and read voraciously. I was a very eager and deeply committed young Christian. Much of what I learned was very helpful and life changing to a degree. But no one ever sat me down and said, "Here are the basics of what you need to know. Here are the fundamental marks of Christian character you need to take on. And here are the non-optional things you need to be doing. And by the way, here are the materials you need to have to go through the process, and I will take you through it."

It is my assessment that if we are not able to begin doing that, our discipleship strategy for the twenty-first century will fail.

So, we have to identify the goals we have for discipleship. What do we want the disciple to know? What do we want him to be? What do we want him to do? If we are not clear on these things, we will never create a compelling discipleship strategy.

In review, we saw in chapter 12, the irreducible minimum of these goals is:

1. Know:
   a. Facts (people, places, events, and chronological order)
   b. Doctrines (major teachings about God, Christ, Holy Spirit, redemption, spiritual growth, spiritual warfare, church, future things, etc.)
   c. Principles (how to pray, discern God's will, live the Christian life, walk in the Spirit, etc.)

d. Problems (What unique problems/challenges does the age group you are discipling have? Peer pressure? Husband/wife relationships? Lust?)

e. Apologetics (What worldview questions does your age group need answered to protect them from attacks on their faith? Existence of God? Evolution? Value of human life? Reliability of Scripture? Credibility of Christian faith?)

2. Be:

a. Love God (demonstrated by trusting and obeying Him)

b. Love others (demonstrated by characteristics of love in 1 Corinthians 13:4–8, and by doing unto others what we would have others do unto us [Luke 6:31]

3. Do:

a. Share faith (giving scriptural truth while telling personal story of salvation)

b. Use spiritual gifts (fulfilling good works God has prepared for us to walk in (Eph. 2:10)

Our task as a discipler is to answer these questions (what do we want our learners to know, be, and do) for the people we are ministering to and to lead them to completeness in each area. You might wish for more detail at this point and to know what curriculum already exists that accomplishes all this. However, going into that would go beyond the scope of this book (see appendix D). But as you carve out your conclusions in each of these areas as best you can, you will grow in your grasp of the task and increase your capacity to lead others.

A deep discipleship strategy will be crystal clear on the goals of discipleship in knowledge, lifestyle, and ministry skill.

Wide: Discipleship Strategy Must Be Complete

The discipleship strategy must also be complete. That is, it must get out to all four corners of the Christian life, targeting all seven marks of a complete Christian:

1. Personal worship

2. Corporate worship

3. Biblical knowledge

4. Christlike lifestyle

5. Ministry skill

6. Impact in the church

7. Impact in the world

> We must assume that whatever gaps exist in our discipleship system will be filled in by a hostile modern culture.

We must assume that whatever gaps exist in our discipleship system will be filled in by a hostile modern culture.

In focusing on the know-be-do components of spiritual growth as being the most demanding challenge of the seven marks, we must be clear that a person's lifestyle will never go beyond his knowledge, and a person's ministry will never go beyond his lifestyle. It is a complete package. Therefore, there is a progression. First, we must establish our knowledge goals and drive them home with groundbreaking effectiveness.

Knowledge Goals: In pursuing our knowledge goals, we must keep in mind that most learning is self-generated. Therefore, we must teach the basics and teach them well. Then, when people have been given a solid foundation in the basics, they are able to build on that foundation and go, through self-directed effort, to whatever heights of learning the Lord leads and enables.

The principles of neurological reconditioning, however, suggest that we typically do not give enough attention to identifying the irreducible minimum of knowledge needed in the Christian life, the importance of burning that knowledge deeply into the memory bank, and reviewing that knowledge regularly so that we easily remember it, and so that it affects our attitudes, values, and behavior. Because we become what we behold, we must behold fundamental truth over and over again to offset the diluting and corrupting impact of the relentless modern culture around us. It is through repetition that knowledge penetrates from the conscious mind to the subconscious mind and converts from intellectual acceptance to deep belief. Until this happens—the conversion of easily remembered truth from intellectual acceptance to deep belief—our knowledge goals have not yet been achieved. Having a basic body of knowledge identified and having repeated exposure to that knowledge until it is deeply memorized is essential to the discipleship process. That is one of the things we are not doing very well.

In my book *30 Days to Understanding the Bible*, I boiled the content down to the irreducible minimum and I used repetition extensively. It is not unusual for me to get an e-mail or comment saying something like, "I thought I was going to croak from filling in the blanks over and over again . . . but by the end of the book, I 'owned' the information on a level I never dreamed I would. Thank you." That is only one small example of an approach that must be used throughout our discipleship experience. And, of course, the methods—all the methods—for teaching when knowledge is the goal (chapter 12) must be used. They work!

Lifestyle Goals: After establishing our knowledge goals and methodology, we must then clarify our lifestyle goals and drive them home

It is through repetition that knowledge penetrates from the conscious mind to the subconscious mind . . .

with groundbreaking effectiveness. We must proceed with the realization that the most powerful methodology we have for influencing a person's attitudes, values, and behavior is the power of our own example. Therefore, the most important methodology we have is the complete commitment of our lives to Christ. Our own focus on our own spiritual growth is the single most important strategy we can employ in attempting to influence others for a Christlike lifestyle.

Our own personal example, however, no matter how powerful, is not the only method we must use to influence the attitudes, values, and behavior of others. We are losing our young people, and we need to try to figure out why. It is not an easy answer, but my assessment is that one reason is because our discipleship strategy is incomplete, having been built on a twentieth-century ministry model.

We often use mediocre knowledge methods and think that we have accomplished lifestyle goals. That is, we teach the content of the Bible (sometimes not very well) and think that is sufficient to guard our children against the power of modern culture. Clearly, it is not. We must pull out the complete arsenal of methods for teaching for lifestyle change (chapter 14) and use them to much greater effectiveness. They work! And, we must begin at an earlier age, before the hormones hit. There is much truth that can be taught and much impact that can be made in younger ages that we often wait until junior high and high school to teach. Many really important things can be taught earlier. This is another of the things we are not doing very well.

Ministry Skill Goals: Finally, we must focus on our ministry skill goals and not rest until our students are sharing their faith and using their spiritual gifts. As we saw in chapter 8, Ephesians 2:10 says, "For we are His workmanship, created in Christ Jesus for good works, which God prepared beforehand that we would walk in them." This verse is telling us that before we were ever born, God created good works that He wants us to do.

God created us to have a need for meaning and purpose in life. And we will never have a sense of meaning and purpose in life until we are doing the things He has prepared for us to do. We must live for something greater than self, or we will begin to turn septic, like the Dead Sea with water flowing in, but nothing flowing out. If we are not doing the good works God prepared for us to walk in, we will begin to look for other things to give us purpose and meaning, and those things are always inferior to serving the Lord. And they often create very negative and harmful behavior patterns. Typically, we turn to the pursuit of pleasure to fill the void.

Therefore, unless we get Christian young people sharing their faith and using their spiritual gifts at an early age, they will be vulnerable to pursuing the same things the world is pursuing to fill the void in their lives. That is why the statistics on attitudes, values, and behavior for Christian young people are often not much better than those for non-Christians.

Again, we fall into the trap of thinking that when we have taught the Bible, we have equipped people for ministry. We have not. We must pull out the arsenal of methods for teaching for ministry skill and use them to much greater effectiveness. They work! Neither are we doing this very well.

Finally, I want to make the point that as we learn, we change, and as we change, we increase our capacity for ministry. It is not that we wait to change until we have learned everything we need to know, and that we do not do anything until we have become all we need to be. Rather, as we learn we change, and as we change we minister. It is incremental across the board.

High: Discipleship Strategy Must Create Spiritual Independence

When children are first born, they are very needy and dependent. They must be taken care of by someone else. They must be fed, cleaned, and protected. Then, as they grow, they begin to feed, clean, and protect themselves. And when they become adults, they are independent, not only able to take care of themselves, but also able to take care of others who need it.

The same is true spiritually. Spiritual infants must be fed, cleaned, and protected. But they must be nurtured in such away that they eventually develop their own independence. There is something terribly wrong with a physical adult who is not able to feed, clean, and protect himself. The same is true with a spiritual adult. So our discipleship strategy must be one that encourages and leads to spiritual independence.

Of course, the better the foundation is laid in knowledge, lifestyle, and ministry skill, the more ready a disciple is to grow to independence.

However, in pointing a disciple to a course of spiritual growth beyond the foundation, we must take into account that lifestyle growth is the single greatest challenge in the Christian experience. In comparison, knowledge and ministry skills are easy. Therefore, the key to spiritual independence is lifestyle growth, and the key to lifestyle growth is mental renewal.

If we use biblical terminology, we speak of being transformed by the renewing of our minds through memorizing and meditating on Scripture. If we use scientific terminology, we speak of neurological reconditioning based on the neuroplasticity of the brain being accomplished through review and repetition. But science is not telling us anything we did not already know from Scripture. It is just telling us how it all works and is reinforcing the vital nature of mental renewal that Paul wrote about two thousand years ago. "Do not be conformed to this world, but be transformed by the renewing of your mind, so that you may prove what the will of God is, that which is good and acceptable and perfect" (Rom. 12:2).

As we have already seen, when we work this passage backward, we see that in order for our lives to be living proof that the will of God is good and acceptable and perfect, we must be transformed, and if we are to be transformed, we must have our minds renewed.

It is all there, the whole spiritual key in a nutshell. If we are to grow in our Christian lifestyle, we must focus on a life of mental renewal. As we not only know (*gnosko*), but really know (*epignosko*) the truth, the truth will set us free (John 8:32)!

As we developed in the previous chapter, Scripture memorization and meditation, as well as guarding the mind by keeping out the bad and letting in the good, are the keys to mental renewal, which is the key to lifestyle transformation.

Therefore, our task as disciplers is to model, teach, and lead a disciple to a lifestyle of mental renewal through Scripture memorization and meditation and carefully to guard the mind to encourage the fruit of the Spirit and discourage the fruit of the flesh (Gal. 5:19–23).

As we do this, we lead the disciple into an open-ended life of spiritual growth that, if built on a deep and wide enough foundation, can go as high as the will of God allows.

We now come to the point that we can graphically summarize the four points of a discipleship system adequate to meet the demands of the twenty-first century.

Brave New Discipleship System

1	When we have identified the irreducible minimum of knowledge, the fundamental marks of lifestyle, and the non-optional ministry abilities for each age group we are ministering to,
2	When we have employed a strategy that covers all the areas of the Christian life with the right methods,
3	When we have modeled and taught a life of ongoing transformation through Scripture-based mental renewal,
4	Then we will have employed an approach to discipleship that can meet the demands of the twenty-first century.

Discipling Yourself Through These Principles

This book has been written from the perspective of discipling others. However, the principles apply equally to self-discipling. If you are not discipling others, you can nevertheless use this book to devise a strategy for guiding and accelerating your own spiritual growth. In fact, even if you are discipling others, you must still be intentional about discipling yourself. As we grow older and more mature, we may not have anyone to disciple us. We may have outgrown our original discipler. Our original discipler may have moved away or died. In either case, whether we are discipling others or not, we need to be alert to the need and opportunities to disciple ourselves, and we can use these principles to do so. I do it all the time.

For example, to help myself learn what I need to know, I am constantly working to maximize memory, understanding, and application. I use the principles for those levels of knowledge to guide my self-education. To increase memory, I may reduce a subject to its irreducible minimum, and then review the information over and over again until I have it memorized. I may create memory devices to help me. As an example, to begin my daily worship time, I use a Scripture prayer process with the acronym M.A.R.K. Those letters introduce a series of Scripture passages that I have woven together into a four-fold prayer: (1) Move toward God, (2) Accept His benevolent intentions toward me, (3) Relinquish myself to His will, and (4) Keep company with Him throughout the day. By recalling these headlines with this memory device, it helps me remember the Scripture prayer that accompanies the headline. I am able to recite a memorized prayer consisting of Scriptures woven together that takes me perhaps five minutes to complete. That is quite a bit of Scripture, which I find I can recall by using the memory device I created.

> . . . to help myself learn what I need to know, I am constantly working to maximize memory, understanding, and application.

If I want to get my mind around the contents of a book so that I understand it better, I underline as I read the book. I refer to this example in chapter 13. Then, when finished, I type up (or now I dictate using voice recognition software) all the underlined parts of the book, creating transitional wording when needed, so that I end up with a tight summary of the book. You recall that summarizing is an excellent way to encourage understanding.

To increase application, I journal, writing out the implications of a truth, observation, or experience to my life. I have hundreds of pages of journaling to this end. I have a single computer file that I use to simply type the date and then make the journal entry about a spiritual, character, or lifestyle issue. It forms a powerful resource for recalling the work of God in my life in times past as fuel for praise and worship as well as inspiration and guidance for His work in the future.

You recall that reading or hearing about individuals who exemplify an attitude, value, or behavior is a powerful way to encourage the cultivaton of those attitudes, values, and behavior in your own life. To that end, I purposefully read books, occasionally watch movies, and do Internet searches on individuals for inspiration to become more tomorrow than I am today. I do character studies in the Scripture and search for similar Scripture passages that I can memorize to help me accelerate growth in a given area of character or lifestyle.

Finally, to advance or create a new ministry skill, I follow the four-step approach outlined in this book. I recently came across a strategy for increasing the amount of information that effectively can be packed into a highly interesting speech or talk. I have seen the process in advance. I am now working on breaking the process down into its parts and practicing it, and I intend to rehearse until I master it.[1]

No matter if you are trying to guide and accelerate your growth in what you know, become, or can do, the principles in this book can be self-applied to help you create a rich and powerful self-discipleship approach for continuously becoming more tomorrow than you are today.

Leading the Way Personally

We saw earlier that in Aldous Huxley's *Brave New World* a very unpleasant future was imagined, not because things people wanted were being withheld from them as was imagined in Orwell's book *1984*, but rather, because everything was given to them. With the glut of things available, regardless of their value, culture and society began to sink to the level of the lowest appetites.

In its broad strokes, this seems to be what is happening in the United States. **Our biblical heritage in the United States is becoming unraveled, and with it, the church is also becoming unraveled.** Pollster George Barna has, over the last twenty or so years, chronicled the unnerving decline of biblical values in American culture, which is paralleled in the church five or ten years later. As disciplers, we must choose to be part of the solution to that problem.

The great issue is, of course, as Aleksandr Solzhenitsyn said in his acceptance speech of the 1983 Templeton Prize, "Men have forgotten God." [2] If that was true in 1983, how much more would it be true today. As a result, truth is now considered relative and individually determined, rather than objective and determined by God. The consequence is that American culture has now replaced truth with feelings and fact with opinions and has joined a mad race to try to find happiness in life by following personal desires.

That, along with the explosion of electronic technology and media that nurtures and fosters that point of view, has resulted in mass entertainment becoming a substitute for a Christian worldview. We are "amusing ourselves to death," as we noted earlier. [3]

If people have nothing to live for at the core of their lives that is greater than themselves, such as pleasing and serving God, they must have something to put at the core to offset the meaninglessness and purposelessness of our post-Christian culture. Today, this vacuum is often filled by a preoccupation with media, since living with the vacuum is often intolerable.

As Augustine observed, "Thou hast made us for Thyself, O Lord, and our hearts are restless until they find their rest in Thee."[4]

Or, as Blaise Pascal more fully observed:

> All men seek happiness. This is without exception. Whatever different means they employ, they all tend to this end. The cause of some going to war and others avoiding it is the same desire in both, attending with different views. The "will" never takes the least step but to this objective. This is the motive of every man, even of those who hang themselves.[5]

Then Pascal went on to say that people try in vain to fill the desire for happiness by whatever they can lay their hands on in the world around them. But these are all inadequate because the "infinite abyss" can only be filled by "an infinite object, that is to say, only by God Himself."[6]

Perhaps the most common thing Americans lay their hands on in today's culture to fill the void in their lives is electronic-based entertainment. That includes sports, television, music, movies, video games, social media, and the Internet with its ever-expanding outlets (computers, tablets, phones, wristwatches, etc.). These things distract us from the emptiness and the purposelessness of much of modern, post-Christian existence.

There is growing research to indicate that for very young children whose brains are still developing, electronic media itself can be a problem in that it keeps children from other activities in the three-dimensional world that stimulate important parts of the brain. But for the sake of this book's content, it is not electronic media itself that is the problem, but the values commonly reflected in electronic media. The pervasiveness of media and the addictive nature of it cause sub-biblical and unbiblical values to wash through our minds over and over again with very powerful impact so that we have many Christians who, on a conscious level, embrace biblical truth but, on a subconscious level, live a lifestyle that denies that truth.

Whatever affects American culture also affects Christians because Christians are part of the world of American culture. No one can help being influenced by the culture in which he lives. That is how God created us, as social beings. This helps us when the culture is good. It hurts us when the culture is bad. American Christians have been slow to perceive or accept the degree to which they are being assimilated into America culture. In leaning over to help the world, we have fallen in.

So a deeply committed Christian must be quick to pick up on the weaknesses of the culture he lives in, realizing that those weaknesses are affecting him. And, he must be equally quick to disciple in a way that takes our culture into account and to help those he is discipling not to be captured by its weaknesses.

The abyss of our personal desires can only be filled by God. To look elsewhere is to take the bait of the enemy. Our task is to accept the demands of discipleship and then disciple out of the power of a changed life, not merely out of a curriculum or strategy.

Dietrich Bonhoeffer famously said, "When Christ calls a man, he bids him come and die."[7]

C. S. Lewis went further:

Christ says, "Give me all. I don't want so much of your time and so much of your money and so much of your work: I want you. I have not come to torment your natural self, but to kill. No half measures are any good. I don't want to cut off a branch here and branch there, I want to have the whole tree down. Hand over the whole natural self . . . I will give you a new self instead. In fact, I will give you Myself: My own will shall become yours."[8]

We will only lead the way as we dedicate ourselves to a life of spiritual excellence. We will set the high-water mark for those under us who will rarely surpass our spiritual example. Therefore, if we are to have significant impact in the world, we must be men and women of significant spiritual stature.

Of course, we do not have to be perfect. People do not expect us to be perfect because they do not want us to expect them to be perfect. But we do have to be committed, and we do have to be growing. Halfhearted measures will always yield halfhearted results. **Our greatest challenge, as well as our greatest opportunity, is to become an example of the Christian life through our single-minded devotion, and on the power of that foundation, give ourselves to the discipleship of others.**

So, let us lead the way both professionally and personally. If we do not do it, who will? Much is at stake. The glory of God, the welfare of individual Christians, the welfare of unreached people, the spiritual trajectory of the church in America, and the impact of Christians worldwide are at stake.

Review for Memory

Leading the Way Professionally

1. Deep: discipleship strategy must have an adequate f_____. (Page 173)

2. Wide: discipleship strategy must be c_____. (Page 177)

3. High: discipleship strategy must create spiritual i_____. (Page 180)

Leading the Way Personally

4. Our biblical heritage in the United States is becoming unraveled, and with it, the c_____ is also becoming unraveled. (Page 185)

5. A deeply committed Christian must be quick to pick up on the w_____ of the culture he lives in, realizing that those weaknesses are affecting him. (Page 187)

6. Our greatest challenge, as well as our greatest opportunity, is to become an e_____ of the Christian life through our single-minded devotion, and on the power of that foundation, give ourselves to the discipleship of others. (Page 188)

Review for Understanding

Summarize this chapter in one hundred words or fewer:

_____

_____

_____

_____

_____

_____

_____

_____

_____

_____

Review for Application

What do you think your greatest challenge is in being able to lead the way professionally? What will you do to meet that challenge?

_____

_____

_____

_____

_____

_____

_____

What do you think your greatest challenge is to being able to lead the way personally? What will you do to meet that challenge?

_____

_____

_____

_____

_____

_____

_____

Appendix A

Brave New Discipleship for the Church

Introduction

This appendix provides a template for evaluating your church's present ministry and can be used to create a complete discipleship system tailor-made for your church. The task is simple, though not easy.

First, read through the Dream, Promise, Steps, Strategy, and Goals for each of the seven ministries of a complete church below.

Second, as you read through the Strategy section, make a list of those things you are already doing and then a list of things you need/ want to start doing.

Third, prioritize and put a time line to the list of things you need to start doing, integrating that with the other six marks of a complete church, creating a master plan for implementation.

The suggestions below are not exhaustive, nor will all of them fit your situation. You may find your church not doing some of the things listed and doing other things not listed. This is intended to be a general guide for a process that will lead a church to the ministry strategy that is best for it.

There Are Key Ministries That Will Facilitate Individual Worship

A rich Christian experience requires a vital inner life. Therefore, the complete Christian sets aside time each day for individual worship and dedicates each activity of his day as an act of worship to God.

The Dream

The dream is to have a church in which people are encouraged and assisted to become faithful in spending time alone with God and in committing every part of their day as an act of worship to Him. Everyone is different, and one size does not fit all, when it comes to individual worship. Therefore, we want to offer a variety of resources to help the individual succeed in this vital life discipline. Ongoing support and reinforcement are essential to having a large percentage of people participating. In addition, we will encourage moving beyond daily quiet times with God, to practicing the presence of God throughout the day as we make every act of the day a gesture of worship to Him.

The Promise

Because we want all our members to worship God individually, our church will facilitate for our members the process of spending daily time with God in His Word and prayer, as well as committing the details of daily life as an act of worship to God with leadership-by-example, resources, and ongoing encouragement.

The Steps

If a mark of a complete Christian is that he worships God individually, then one ministry of a complete church is that it facilitates the believer worshiping God individually. Two things are important in encouraging church members to worship God individually.

1. **Create a Culture.** The first is to create a culture in which individual worship is championed by those in leadership. The leaders must model individual worship, they must talk about it, they must champion it, and they must give examples, tell stories, and give testimonies of benefit that has come to their lives through their own individual worship. In addition, they must be models

of living one's entire life in service to God with each daily activity being an act of worship to Him.

2. **Facilitate Worship.** The second is to facilitate individual worship by teaching people how to worship individually and providing resources and guidance for doing so and offering ongoing encouragement.

The Strategy: Basic Individual Worship Program

1. Provide instruction, which every person in the church is encouraged to take at least once, that provides biblical direction and encouragement for individual worship, and encourage all new attendees to take the course as part of their initiation into the church.

2. Provide devotional materials and individual worship guides promoted at the beginning of each new year and reinforced and encouraged throughout the year.

3. Provide testimonies of leaders in the church at the beginning of the new year, and throughout the year, regarding the value and/ or details of their individual worship.

The Goal

The goal is to have the majority of regular attendees experience a meaningful daily devotional time, as well as pray and meditate on Scripture throughout the day as they consciously live each part of each day as an act of worship to God.

There Are Key Ministries That Will Inspire Corporate Worship

The Christian life was never meant to be lived alone. Therefore, the complete Christian worships God with other Christians and integrates his entire life with other Christians.

The Dream

The dream is to have a church in which corporate worship is significantly enriched because individuals are also involved in personal worship during the week and have committed their whole lives to worship. The dream is that worship be God-centered, not human-centered, reflecting the fact that in worship we are not the audience, with ministers and musicians the performers. Rather, the worshipers are the performers, and God is the audience. The dream is for corporate worship to be a true expression of an authentic relationship with God, based on personal holiness, calling public attention to the greatness of who God is and what He has done for us. It is a time when one believer joins with other believers to raise their expression of devotion to a higher level than can be achieved alone. In addition, these fellow worshipers integrate their entire lives with other Christians.

The Promise

Because we all need to worship God corporately, our church is a place where members are inspired to participate in meaningful, well-planned corporate worship experiences and are encouraged and helped to integrate their everyday lives with other believers.

The Steps

If a mark of a complete Christian is that he worships God corporately, then one ministry of a complete church is that it inspires the believer to worship God corporately. Two things are important in inspiring church members to worship God corporately.

1. **Create a Culture.** The first is to create a culture in which corporate worship is championed by those in leadership. Several extremes must be avoided. One extreme, an increasingly old fashioned one, is one in which the sermon is everything and all else is nothing. In some churches, everything but the sermon is considered the preliminaries. Some old timers do not even come to the singing ahead of time but show up just in time to hear the sermon. That culture denigrates worship. The other extreme, an increasingly modern one, is one in which entertainment is everything. If the music and sermon are not professional quality, the people will not come. Sunday morning has the feel of a performance rather than a gathering of God's people for corporate worship. The balance point is where both are important, and both are done authentically, worshiping in spirit and in truth (John 4:24)

2. **Inspire Corporate Worship.** The second is to inspire corporate worship by teaching people how to worship corporately and by providing opportunities for corporate worship. The teaching could be ongoing, spontaneous teaching from the pulpit and during worship services, as well as a concentrated and formal time of instruction on the biblical principles of corporate worship. The opportunities would include Sunday morning, of course, and other times when corporate worship is the focus.

The Strategy: Basic Corporate
Worship Program

1. Provide instruction, which every person in the church is encouraged to take once, that provides instruction on the biblical principles of corporate worship, and encourage all new attendees to take this course as part of their initiation into the church.

2. Reinforce instruction and encouragement spontaneously throughout the year. Conduct weekly worship services that are carefully

planned and executed with a high view of biblical corporate worship.

3. Encourage Christians to be involved in one another's lives throughout the week, and provide opportunities to do so.

The Goal

The goal is to have the majority of regular attendees meaningfully involved in regular corporate worship services and meaningfully integrated into the lives of other Christians.

There Are Key Ministries That Will Instruct in Biblical Knowledge

Knowledge is not everything, but everything rests on knowledge. Therefore, the complete Christian commits to mastering the Bible so well that the Bible masters him.

The Dream

The dream is to have a church where the Bible is valued and taught effectively from the pulpit and small group contexts. The dream is for Scripture to permeate the thoughts, attitudes, values, and behavior of the congregation so that the faith and life of the congregation brings glory to God and rich blessing to the people.

The Promise

Because we need to learn biblical truth, our church is a place where the Bible is preached effectively from the pulpit and taught in small group contexts and where members are encouraged and helped to master the Bible well enough for it to penetrate their thinking, values, attitudes, and behavior and to guide them in their decisions.

The Steps

If the mark of a complete Christian is that he is mature in his knowledge of biblical truth, then one ministry of a complete church is that it instructs the believer in biblical knowledge. Two things are important in instructing members in biblical knowledge.

1. **Create a Culture.** The first is to create a culture in which biblical instruction is championed by those in leadership. The Bible must be seen as the inerrant word of God and the supreme authority in matters of faith and life and appealed to when determining church vision, priorities, and ministry.

2. **Instruct in Biblical Knowledge**. The second is to further Bible knowledge by placing Bible teaching at the center of ministry in the church and by paying the price, both in finances and human resources, to offer systematic instruction through all grade levels in the church.

The Strategy: Basic Biblical Instruction

1. Commit to a basic Bible knowledge curriculum for the church and aspire to have all members participate in it to lead them to a systematic and progressively mature knowledge of Scripture.

2. Commit to ministry structures, such as adult Sunday school, home Bible studies, and various other seminar-based and retreat-based contexts in which Scripture can be effectively taught.

The Goal

The goal is to create a system of Bible instruction into which all members are encouraged to enter. Promote it as a central feature of the life and ministry of the church and a foundation for all other ministry in the church.

There Are Key Ministries That Will Nurture a Christlike Lifestyle

A Christian is measured not primarily by what he knows or what he does but by who he is. Therefore, a complete Christian commits to being conformed to the character image of Christ.

The Dream

The dream is to have a church where people are nurtured in mature Christian character, bringing their lives into increasing conformity to the character and behavior of Christ. As a result, they do not bring unnecessary pain into their own lives, and they are able to guide their children and others into an abundant personal life, creating an effective testimony of the power of God's truth to those who have not yet received Him.

The Promise

Because we need to become persons of exemplary character, the church will offer the nurture and assistance necessary for personal spiritual growth, including fellowship, small groups, spiritual accountability relationships, mentoring, and intentional discipleship.

The Steps

If the mark of a complete Christian is that he is mature in his character, then one ministry of a complete church is that it nurtures the believer in Christlike character. Two things are important in inspiring church members to Christlike character.

1. **Create a Culture.** The first is to create a culture in which Christlike character is championed by those in leadership. Christlike character must be seen as the central measure of the Christian life, realizing that a person may know the Bible well and still not be a person of exemplary character.

2. **Nurture in Christlike Lifestyle.** The second is to further Christlike character by initiating a comprehensive nurture ministry throughout the church. The nurture ministry should focus on all five key areas of a person's life—the personal area, the family, the church, work, and society.

The Strategy: Basic Nurture in Christlike Lifestyle

1. Initiate a church-wide nurturing program on a basic level, for new Christians or for Christians who have not had a nurturing church background. This could include fellowship activities, small groups, spiritual accountability relationships, mentoring, and intentional discipleship.

2. Promote biblical character traits throughout various venues in the church, including testimonies during the worship service, the bulletin, newsletter, posters, and bulletin boards.

The Goal

The goal is to create a system of nurture into which all members are encouraged to enter. Promote it as a central feature of the life and ministry of the church and a key component with all other ministry in the church.

There Are Key Ministries That Will Train in Ministry Skills

Each Christian is given a job to do and gifts to do it with. Therefore, a complete Christian discovers and uses his spiritual gifts and shares his faith with others.

The Dream

The dream is to have a church where people will know their spiritual gifts and serve eagerly in areas that bring meaning and satisfaction to them. In this way, the needs of the church can be met by those who are gifted to meet them and who take great meaning in doing so. In addition, they are trained to be able to share their faith as a natural part of their everyday lives, bringing satisfaction and reward to them and providing an army of people to share their faith and bringing into the church new Christians.

The Promise

Because we need to learn how to serve others, the church will train people how to identify and develop their spiritual gifts and how to effectively share their faith with others.

The Steps

If the mark of a complete Christian is that he is skilled in his ministry abilities, the church will train the believer to identify his spiritual gifts and share his faith. Two things are important in inspiring church members to Christlike character.

1. **Create a Culture.** The first is to create a culture in which skilled service is championed by those in leadership. The employment of ministry skills must be seen as a logical and unavoidable result of growing in knowledge and character. If a person is not yet ministering to others through evangelism and through his spiritual gifts, there is still something that person does not know, or there is an area of spiritual growth that he has not yet experienced. A non-serving Christian is still an incomplete Christian. The leaders in the church both promote and model these values. If they are not modeling these values, they will very likely not happen in the church. The primary issue here is evangelism. If the pastor

or pastors are not conspicuously involved in evangelism, it is not likely that the members of the congregation will be either.

2. **Train in Ministry Skill.** The second is to further ministry skill training by initiating a comprehensive ministry skill training throughout the church. The ministry skill training should focus both on spiritual gift training and evangelism training.

The Strategy: Basic Ministry Training

1. Provide spiritual gift assessment and foundational ministry preparation and training, helping the Christian understand what kinds of ministries use his spiritual gifts and facilitating entry points for beginning new ministry.

2. Provide basic evangelism training as a central ministry that everyone in the church is urged to participate in.

The Goal

Create training courses that prepare individuals for active involvement in ministries for which they are gifted and for evangelism so that the church achieves the goal of every member being a minister.

There Are Key Ministries That Will Mobilize for Ministry in the Church

Christians are family and should care for one another. Therefore, the complete Christian uses his time, talent, and treasure for the welfare of the church and other Christians.

The Dream

The dream is to have a church where people are committed to serving part of the body of Christ that they are physically part of. This means mobilizing Christians to support their church financially and with their talents. In turn, the church will be mobilized to help the individual financially, if necessary, and with its talents. The goal is a church that grows to maturity in Christ because all the members are committed to the welfare of the others. The goal is to create a community in which practical unity reflects the spiritual unity underlying it.

The Promise

Because Christians are family and should care for one another, the church will equip and mobilize members to look out for the welfare of other Christians and have them look out for each member.

The Steps

If the mark of a complete Christian is that he is committed to serve his church, the church will mobilize the believer to impact his church. Two things are important in mobilizing members to impact the church.

1. **Create a Culture.** The first is to create a culture in which service in the church with one's talents and treasures is a value. It is expected when a person becomes a member of the church that he is committing his talents and treasure to the church. If he is not ready to do that, he is not ready to become a member. Since churches usually get what they expect, this expectation must become part of the culture of the church from the membership class on.

2. **Mobilize for Impact.** The second is to mobilize members for impact in the church by creating the expectation that people give and serve, as well as by creating the infrastructure for getting people involved from the beginning.

The Strategy: Basic Mobilization

1. Create a sermon series to promote the value of serving the church with one's time, talent, and treasure.

2. Create a membership class in which service and support for the church are presented as expectations of membership.

3. Offer an annual ministry fair to acquaint people with possible avenues for service.

The Goal

The goal is to create opportunities to challenge and guide individuals into service for the church, both in terms of financial support as well as volunteering for ministry in the church.

There Are Key Ministries That Will Deploy for Ministry to the World

Because God loved the world and gave Himself for it (John 3:16), so should the church. Therefore, the complete Christian serves the world through evangelism and humanitarianism.

The Dream

The dream is to have a church where people are trained and deployed to share the good news of Jesus, whether it be in their workplace, their neighborhood, or around the world. The goal is personal involvement as well as cross-cultural missions. In addition, the dream is to have a church where people are deployed to help those in need and to be a light of the gospel in a darkened world by doing what they can to help make the world a better place. When Christians help meet the practical needs of people, it not only helps make the world a better place, but also prepares people's hearts to hear the gospel of Christ.

The Promise

Because Christians must love the world as God did, the church will deploy its people for ministry to the world through evangelism and humanitarianism.

The Steps

If the mark of a complete Christian is that he is committed to minister to the world, the church will deploy the believer to impact the world. Two things are important in deploying church members to minister to the world.

1. **Create a Culture.** The first is to create a culture in which ministry to the world is a value. It is expected when a person becomes a member of the church that he is committing himself to ministering to the world through evangelism and humanitarianism.

2. **Deploy for Impact.** The second is to deploy members for impact to the world by creating the expectation that people get involved, as well as by creating the infrastructure for getting people involved from the moment of membership, if not before.

The Strategy: Basic Deployment

1. Provide basic evangelism training, which involves actual evangelism as part of the process.

2. Provide basic instruction in humanitarianism, and sponsor basic humanitarian projects in which members can get involved. Take up benevolence offerings regularly so that the church can respond to benevolence requests when they come, and then tell stories to the church of how their benevolence offering impacted lives.

The Goal

The goal is to create opportunities to challenge and guide individuals into ministry to the world, both in evangelism and humanitarianism.

Appendix B
Brave New Discipleship for Christian Schools
and Homeschools

The information in this book can be a powerful resource for homeschools and for Christian schools and colleges if there is a desire in those institutions for intentional discipleship as part of the school's ministry.

Discipleship Responsibility

To review, this book states that there are three mandates for a Christian:

1. Worship
2. Grow
3. Impact

These three mandates can be expanded into seven to see the issues more clearly:

Worship
1. Individually
2. Corporately

Grow
3. Biblical knowledge
4. Christlike lifestyle
5. Ministry skill

Impact
6. Church
7. World

These identify the seven marks of a complete Christian and determine the seven ministries of a complete church. Because a Christian school is not a church, the school does not need to accept responsibility for all seven marks. Primary attention could be focused on the Grow component, including biblical knowledge, Christlike lifestyle, and ministry skill. All three of those would be in the bull's-eye of a discipleship strategy in Christian education.

Strategic Planning Questions

When a school targets those three discipleship goals—knowledge, lifestyle, and ministry skill—it must then ask and answer six questions for each student age group:

1. What is our goal (what do we want them to know, be, and do)?

2. What is our strategy (how will we accomplish this)?

3. What is our evaluation tool (how will we know when we have been successful)?

4. Who is our personnel (who will do what in the strategy)?

5. What are our methods (what methods will we use, and do they match our goals)?

6. What are our materials (what curriculum will we use to implement)?

Each of those six questions must be answered for each age group in the school: grades 1–3, grades 4–6, grades 7–8, and grades 9–12. We would ask, "What do we want our elementary school children grades 1–3 to know, be, and do as a result of going through our school? How will we get them to know, be, and do this? How will we know when we have been successful? Who will implement the strategy? What methods will they use for each goal? And what material/curriculum will we use?" Then, the same six-step process would continue through each age group through high school.

The answers to those six questions, when implemented, can guide a Christian school into an effective discipleship ministry. Home-schoolers can do the same for their children.

Now, let us explore the six strategic planning questions for additional detail.

What Is Our Goal?

This question must be answered on an age-appropriate level. That is, what you want a first grader to know will be quite different than what you want a twelfth grader to know. Then, the goals must be answered from a holistic level. That is, what you want a sixth grader to know must be integrated with what you want him/her to know as a first grader and twelfth grader.

For example, you may want a first grader to know the facts of the Bible, but on a very basic level. As a sixth grader, you may teach additional facts, but on a more detailed and complete level, relying on what he/she was taught as a first grader. And, of course, the same would be true of a twelfth grader. All that to say, the question of what you want your student to know must be answered on an age-appropriate level, taking into account what the student may have already learned and what he/she may have yet to learn.

Of course, this would be true of lifestyle and ministry skill goals as well. What we expect a first grader to be and do is quite different from what we expect of a twelfth grader.

What Is Our Strategy?

This next question addresses the issue of how you will accomplish the discipleship goal. That is, if you want your twelfth graders to know the facts, doctrines, principles, problems, and apologetics appropriate to their age level, how will you teach them that information?

Most likely, the Bible curriculum can be adjusted to accomplish the knowledge goals. However, the lifestyle goals are not easily accomplished in a Bible curriculum, because the methodology for lifestyle goals is different from the methodology for knowledge goals. As a result, the school is likely to need to establish a mentoring strategy that involves extracurricular or cocurricular activities.

If a certain methodology is used, chapel programs can be used for lifestyle goals. The same with assemblies, or non-chapel meetings. This would not be sufficient by itself, however, so a life-on-life mentoring system may need to be established. Perhaps the students could be assigned to teachers who would assume responsibility for mentoring them. Of course, this would not eliminate the need for all teachers to informally mentor all students. That is one of the great strengths of Christian education. But one faculty member could be assigned a segment of students for which he would be accountable for certain mentoring responsibilities.

Exactly how the lifestyle goal would be addressed would be unique to each school. But if the goal is understood and embraced, an effective way to meet it can be discovered.

The ministry skill goals might be met partially in a classroom situation and partially in an outside-the-classroom situation. That is, certain information could be presented in the classroom, but then the guided rehearsal of the skill might need to happen outside the classroom. Again, where it happens is not as important as using the proper methodology.

What Is Our Evaluation Tool?

The evaluation tools for knowledge are relatively easy. Usually tests and grades are given for knowledge goals.

Lifestyle goals are much more subtle and complex. Participation requirements in lifestyle activities can be part of the evaluation process, but of course, all that will measure is participation. It will not measure internal change. For that, a combination of self-assessment can be used, where the student evaluates himself/herself on personal change, as well as gentle assessment on the part of mentors.

Ministry skill goals tend to be in between knowledge and lifestyle goals in ease of assessment. In some cases, the evaluation can be tested. For example, if a student is required to learn the Romans Road (verses in Romans that can be used to lead someone to Christ), that can be tested, like any knowledge exam. Then, the use of that knowledge in a role-playing situation, in which the student shares his faith and the truth of Scripture with another student, can be assessed on a more subjective level by a faculty member or parent volunteer.

Who Will Implement the Strategy?

With knowledge goals, this will usually be obvious. It will be the Bible teachers. In the lifestyle goals, it may not be so obvious. The strategy for the lifestyle goals might include a combination of faculty, parent volunteers, older students, a chaplain, youth ministers in the area, parachurch ministries, and so on. The same might be true of ministry skill goals.

What Methods Will Be Used to Implement the Strategy?

This is a critical issue. A wide representation of all the appropriate methods for a given goal (chapters 13 and 14) must be used if the goal is to be consistently and effectively reached. The great danger is falling back to the thinking that if we have taught someone information in a classroom situation, then the goal has been achieved. And in the case of knowledge goals, that might be correct. But the danger is falling back on knowledge methods to achieve lifestyle and ministry skill goals. This is a common and significant failure. Someone must be given responsibility and authority to ensure that correct methods are being used effectively for each of the three goals. This might be an administrator, a chaplain, or a department chair. But the buck must stop on someone's desk, or consistent quality control is unlikely to be achieved.

What Materials Will Be Used to Implement the Strategy?

This addresses the issue of curriculum. It may be that existing curriculum will accomplish some of the goals, though the curriculum may need to be taught using different methods.

When mentoring students, extracurricular materials might be used, such as discipleship curriculum for local churches, and so on.

There may be times when curriculum may have to be created by faculty in order to achieve stated goals.

These six questions were answered as they relate to a Christian school. However, with a little creativity and ingenuity, the same goals can be accomplished by homeschool families. Resources and cooperation among co-op families and other sources can help achieve the discipleship goals.

Strategic Planning Questions: Discipleship Template

The following is an outline of the above process and information to aid in getting a bird's-eye view.

I. What are our discipleship goals for our students as a result of going through our school?
   A. Know
      1. Facts of the Bible (people, places, events, chronological order, etc.)
      2. Doctrines of the Bible (main ones agreed upon)
      3. Principles of Christian Living (how to live the Christian life)
      4. Problems (common age-specific problems students face)
      5. Apologetics (answers to common questions that threaten the faith)

B. Be
  1. Love of God (manifested by faithful obedience to Scripture)
  2. Love of our neighbor (manifested by doing unto others what we would have others do unto us)
C. Do
  1. Evangelism (sharing our faith with others)
  2. Humanitarianism (being a good Samaritan to others)

II. What is our strategy for accomplishing this?
  A. Know: Teach (curriculum, Bible, etc.)
  B. Be: Mentor (mentoring relationships, self-evaluation projects, discipleship activities, etc.)
  C. Do: Train (local, USA, and international service projects, etc.)

III. How will we know when we have arrived?
  A. Know: Test grades, and so on
  B. Be: Self-evaluation process, reports from mentoring activities
  C. Do: Record of activity in projects

IV. Who will do this?
  A. Know: Bible teachers
  B. Be: Discipleship system mentors
  C. Do: Project personnel and volunteers

V. What methods will be used?
  A. Know: Classroom teaching
  B. Be: Mentoring relationships
  C. Do: Internships, projects, and trips

VI. What materials will be needed?
  A. Existing texts and discipleship materials
  B. May need to write/create some material
  C. Cooperate with other ministries

Strategic Planning Chart

The following is the same information as above but reduced into a chart form. The chart can easily be used as a checklist for implementing a complete discipleship strategy.

Strategic Planning Chart
Brave New Discipleship System

Grade	Goal	Strategy	Evaluation	Personnel	Methods	Materials
1–3 4–6 7–8 9–12	**Know** • Facts • Doctrines • Principles • Problems • Apologetics	• Bible • Curriculum • (Specifics?)	• Tests/projects • (Specifics?)	• Bible teachers • (Specifics?)	• Classroom instruction • (Specifics?)	• (Specifics?)
	Be • Character (Love God) • Behavior (Love others)	• Mentoring • Activities/self-evaluation projects • (Specifics?)	• Participation, self-evaluation • (Specifics?)	• Mentoring staff • (Specifics?)	• Mentoring relationships • Activities • (Specifics?)	• (Specifics?)
	Do • Share Faith • Use Gifts	• Training activities, service projects • (Specifics?)	• Participation, self-evaluation • (Specifics?)	• Project volunteers • (Specifics?)	• Projects/trips • (Specifics?)	• (Specifics?)

When these six questions are effectively answered and implemented, they will create a complete discipleship strategy for Christian schools and home schools.

Appendix C
Brave New Discipleship Curriculum

ome years ago I was teaching in the doctor of ministry (DMin)
program in a seminary on the West Coast. In order to be
enrolled in a DMin program, students must have had a certain number of years in the ministry, and these students were seasoned pastors.

I taught them much of the information in this book. After the
course was over, one of the pastors came up to me and said, "This
course was really good, but it was the single most frustrating course
I have ever taken." Surprised, I asked why. He replied, "Because you
have shown me what I need to do in my church, but the materials
package to do it doesn't exist."

That was correct, but I suggested that he could go to Christian
bookstores and other publishing resources to find the materials that
are closest to what is needed. I told him that sometimes I had to write
my own material.

He responded intensely that he did not have the time or expertise
to do either. He said, "You need to write this material!"

I chuckled and said that I could not do that. He asked why. I said,
"Because I already have a full-time job."

"Then quit your job!" he rejoined.

At first, I thought he was kidding, but then it became clear that he
was not. His response was a heartfelt plea.

I knew the feeling. I had wanted a total curriculum package to
implement myself and knew that it did not exist. Even I was frustrated
that I had to pore over existing material to try to choose the best for
what I wanted to accomplish. And often enough I could not find what
I wanted. But there was no other option.

That was a couple of decades ago. In the fullness of God's timing, I have now written the core curriculum. It is called *The Brave New Discipleship System*. It follows all the principles that I have outlined in these pages. I have started with the most basic level of discipleship and will progress as far as the will of God determines.

To preview the material, visit www.bravenewdiscipleship.com. That web address is the home of additional discipleship resources and strategies that you may find helpful as well. For still other resources, visit my blog at www.maxanders.com.

Appendix D

Use of Media vs. People in Discipleship

As we rethink discipleship methods for the twenty-first century, it automatically raises the question as to whether, and how much, we use electronic media in the discipleship process. The transition of American culture from a print-based culture to an electronic media-based culture demands that we make a clear-headed decision about whether or not to make the same transition in our discipleship process.

Electronic media and the Internet are here to stay. In fact, their presence and influence will only increase as time goes on. Therefore, a forward-thinking Christian must find a way to embrace this reality and make it work for the kingdom. We must either pull away from the world to protect ourselves, or use the same technology and methodology that tend to draw people away from Christ to draw them to Christ.

Yet to say that introduces a danger, namely, that we will increasingly use video, but in an unhelpful way, or in such a way that it does not accomplish the overall goal of discipleship. Most current Christian video material is either a talking-head format (video of an individual talking to the camera or to someone just off camera or of a sermon being preached or seminar being conducted) or a movie format.

There is nothing wrong with either of those formats. But those formats are limited in educational scope and discipleship impact. Those formats by themselves cannot lead a person to maturity in Christ, because they do not contain the breadth of ministry experiences necessary to become mature in Christ. Nor do they contain the full spectrum of methods that must be used in order to lead someone to maturity in Christ.

The talking-head format is essentially a lecture, having the same limitations as a sermon, which is best at explaining or inspiring. The movie format is best at storytelling, which allows us to see people who exemplify, inspire, motivate, and model desired behavior.

This is all potentially good as far as it goes, but it is not a complete offering for discipleship and cannot, by itself, lead a person to maturity in Christ. Because a disciple must know, be, and do, there is a full spectrum of methods that were overviewed in chapters 13 and 14 that must be employed if those three goals are to be reached.

In addition, work with pen and paper is also important to the spiritual growth process. While video can be a part of the process, it cannot be the entire process. The brain does not work that way. Some reading and writing must follow video, or the impact of the video will be very short-lived.

For that reason, any video-based approach to discipleship must be complete, addressing know, be, and do goals, and must use the methods appropriate to those goals. This is a massive undertaking, but one that must be accomplished if we are to meet the demands of discipleship in our Brave New World.

The basic discipleship system I have created, *The Brave New Discipleship System*, is DVD-based, accompanied by a learner's manual in which written exercises are completed after viewing the video. It is my conviction that the two together—video and learner's manual—compose the most powerful learning experience. Let me tell you why.

When I started working on this discipleship system, I assumed it would be a series of books similar to the ones I have already written. However one day, through the leading of the Lord, I took a simple idea from the material I had already written and created a short video out of it, using eye-popping visuals and stirring music. When I finished and hit the play button to view my work, to my surprise, I wept.

I thought to myself, *What is going on here? I didn't weep when I wrote it. Why did I weep when I watched it?* I began researching how the brain works and learned that the left side of our brain is the systematic and logical side, while the right side is the creative and emotional side. When I wrote the material for the video, it was a left-brained exercise. When I added pictures and music to it, it added a right-brained experience. I learned that an educational experience that combines left-brained activity with right-brained activity is the most complete and most powerful learning experience. The words tell us what to believe while the music and pictures tell us how to feel about what we believe. The pictures and music intensify the truth of the words, helping us grasp more fully the significance of the truth and drive that truth more deeply into the heart and mind.

I concluded that the curriculum I was embarking on had to include video.

The Brave New Discipleship system addresses all three ministry goals (know, be, and do) with methodology consistent with those goals, including carefully created exercises to be done in the workbook, which cement in the learner's mind the information in the video. It is a powerful and complete learning experience.

At the same time that we make the case for using video in the discipleship process, it must be stressed that video itself is not the whole answer. We still need life-on-life mentoring. In the list of methods for helping a person become what he was meant to be (in chapter 14), life-on-life is the single most powerful influence. So, to relegate discipleship exclusively to video-based courses is to put a lid on discipleship, capping the process to eliminate the most powerful influence of one person on another person. We do not want to do that. Life-on-life discipleship should always be used and encouraged and should be seen as the method with the greatest impact and most potential to impact attitudes, values, and behavior.

However, imagine that you had led someone to Christ and wanted to disciple that person. It would still be your responsibility to lead the person to a basic knowledge of Christian truth. It would still be your responsibility to help the person become what he/she needs to become and do what he/she needs to do, at first on a basic level, and then on a more advance level. You would need some kind of material or curriculum to accomplish that.

The Brave New Discipleship System includes a comprehensive basic survey of truth needed in the Christian life, along with exercises to guide and accelerate life-change and ministry skill development. The video-based curriculum along with the opportunity to develop strong personal relationships with people you are leading through the material create a powerful opportunity to influence people deeply for Christ.

The Brave New Discipleship material does not complete the Christian, however. Rather, it starts the Christian. It is not the most a Christian needs to know, be, and do. It is the least. It is not the end of discipleship. It is only the beginning. However, it establishes a strong foundation for self-generated learning. With that foundation, the disciple can profit from additional discipleship material and mentoring relationships. This material is not designed to replace any other discipleship or educational ministries of the church. Rather, it is designed to provide a foundation—an undergirding—to make them even more effective.

Notes

Chapter 1

1. Dallas Willard, *The Divine Conspiracy* (New York: HarperCollins Publishers, 1997), 58.

Chapter 2

1. Peggy Noonan, *Life, Liberty and the Pursuit of Happiness* (New York: Random House, 1994), 64.

2. Ibid., 65.

3. Ibid., 64, 67.

4. Mary Pipher, *The Shelter of Each Other* (New York: Ballentine Books, 1996), 13–15.

5. Neil Postman, *Amusing Ourselves to Death*, rev. ed. (New York: Penguin Books, 2005).

6. Francis Schaeffer, *How Should We Then Live?* (Old Tappan, NJ: Fleming H. Revell, 1976), 20.

Chapter 3

1. G. R. Stephenson, "Cultural Acquisition of a Specific Learned Response among Rhesus Monkeys," in Progress in Primatology, ed. D. Starek, R. Schneider, and H. J. Kuhn (Stuttgart: Fischer, 1967), 279–88.

2. George Barna, *Index of Leading Spiritual Indicators* (Nashville: Thomas Nelson, 1996), 80, 98.

Chapter 4

1. William J. Cromie, "Meditation Changes Temperatures: Mind Controls Body in Extreme Experiments," *Harvard University Gazette*, April 18, 2002, http://news.harvard.edu/gazette/2002/04.18/09-tummo.html.

2. John McCain and Mark Salter, *Faith of My Fathers* (New York: HarperCollins Publishers, 2008), 206.

3. "Mr. Pennington's Machine," *The Lloyd Bridges Show*, IMDb, http://www.imdb.com/title/tt0634302/.

4. Peggy Noonan, *Life, Liberty and the Pursuit of Happiness* (New York: Random House, 1994), 215.

5. Joseph M. Stowell, *Eternity: Reclaiming a Passion for What Endures* (Grand Rapids: Discovery House, 2006), 7.

6. Dallas Willard, *The Spirit of the Disciplines* (San Francisco: Harper and Row, 1988), 7.

7. Ibid., 3.

8. Gordon MacDonald, *The Life God Blesses* (Nashville: Thomas Nelson, 1994), 70–71.

Chapter 5

1. *2001: A Space Odyssey.* Directed by Stanley Kubrick. Screenplay by Stanley Kubrick and Arthur C. Clark. 1968. Los Angeles: Metro-Goldwyn-Mayer. It is based on the short story "The Sentinel" by Arthur C. Clark.

2. C. S. Lewis, *Letters of C. S. Lewis* (San Diego: Harcourt Brace, 1993), 224.

3. C. S. Lewis, *God in the Dock* (New York: HarperCollins Publishers, 1970), 62.

4. C. S. Lewis, *Surprised by Joy* (New York: Harcourt, Brace and Jovanovich, 1955), 228.

5. James Packer, *God Has Spoken* (Grand Rapids: Baker Book House, 1993), 50.

6. Harold Kushner, *When All You Ever Wanted Isn't Enough* (New York: Fireside, 2002), 166.

Chapter 6

1. John R. W. Stott, *Your Mind Matters* (Downers Grove: InterVarsity Press, 1972), 60.

Chapter 7

1. Charles Colson, *Loving God* (Grand Rapids: Zondervan, 1983), 92.

2. C. S. Lewis, *Mere Christianity,* (Grand Rapids: Zondervan, 1952), 204–205.

Chapter 8

1. Max Anders, *What You Need to Know about the Holy Spirit* (Nashville: Thomas Nelson, 1995), 86.

2. Harold Kushner, *When All You Ever Wanted Isn't Enough* (New York: Fireside, 2002), 18.

3. James Packer, *Evangelism and the Sovereignty of God* (Downers Grove: InterVarsity Press, 1961), 91.

Chapter 9

1. Harold Kushner, *When All You Ever Wanted Isn't Enough* (New York: Fireside, 2002), 59.

2. Randy Alcorn, *The Treasure Principle* (Sisters, OR: Multnomah, 2001), 17.

3. Elisabeth Elliot, *The Shadow of the Almighty* (NewYork: Harper and Row, 1958), 108.

4. Hugh Hewitt, *In, but Not Of* (Nashville: Thomas Nelson, 2003), 148.

Chapter 10

1. D. James Kennedy, *What If Jesus Had Never Been Born?* (Nashville: Thomas Nelson, 2001).

2. Ibid., 92.

3. David N. Livingstone, "Where Would Civilization Be Without Christianity? The Gift of Science," *Christianity Today,* December 6, 1999, http://www.christianitytoday.com /ct/1999/december6/9te052.html.

4. Greg Laurie, *The Upside Down Church* (Wheaton: Tyndale House Publishers, 1999), 91.

Chapter 12

1. Educational resources: Benjamin S. Bloom, ed., *A Taxonomy of Educational Objectives*, book 1, *Cognitive Domain* (New York: Longman, 1956); David R. Krathwohl, Benjamin S. Bloom, and Bertram B. Masia, *A Taxonomy of Educational Objectives*, book 2, *Affective Domain* (New York: Longman, 1965); James H. Block, *Mastery Learning: Theory and Practice* (New York; Holt, Rinehard and Winston, 1971).

2. Leroy Ford, *Design for Teaching and Training* (Nashville: Broadman Press, 1978).

Chapter 13

1. Lynne M. Reder and John R. Anderson, "Effects of Spacing and Embellishment on Memory for the Main Points of a Text," *Memory and Cognition* 10, no. 2 (1982): 97–102.

Chapter 14

1. Daniel Defoe, *Robinson Crusoe* (London: Seeley, Service, & Co. 1919).

2. James Dobson, *What Wives Wish Their Husbands Knew about Women* (Carol Stream, IL: Tyndale, 1975).

Chapter 16

1. From a Nike commercial, which can be viewed at: https://www.youtube.com/watch?v=45mMioJ5szc.

2. Carolyn Gregoire, "The Brain-Training Secrets of Olympic Athletes," *The Huffington Post*, February 11, 2014, http://www.huffingtonpost.com/2014/02/11/mind-hacks-from-olympic-a_n_4747755.html.

3. Ibid.

4. Carl Zimmer, "Secrets of the Brain," *National Geographic*, 225, no. 1 (February 2014): 28–57.

5. Barry Gordon, "Can We Control Our Thoughts? Why Do Thoughts Pop into My Head as I'm Trying to Fall Asleep?" *Scientific American*, February 14, 2013, http://www.scientificamerican.com/article/can-we-control-our-thoughts/.

6. Benedict Carey, "Who's Minding the Mind?" *New York Times*, July 31, 2007, http://www.nytimes.com/2007/07/31/health/psychology/31subl.html?pagewanted=all&_r=0.

7. http://web.stanford.edu/group/hopes/cgi-bin/wordpress/2010/06/neuroplasticity/.

8. Ibid.

9. Gary Smalley, *Change Your Heart, Change Your Life* (Nashville: Thomas Nelson, 2007), 41–42

10. Ibid., 26.

Chapter 17

1. Carmine Gallo, *Talk Like TED* (New York: St. Martin Press, 2014).

2. Aleksandr Solzhenitsyn, "Godlessness: The First Step to the Gulag" (lecture, Templeton Prize, London, May 10, 1983).

3. Neil Postman, *Amusing Ourselves to Death*, rev. ed. (New York: Penguin Books, 2005).

4. www.inumc.org/newsdetail/422869.

5. Blaise Pascal, *Pascal's Pensees*, trans. W. F. Trotter (New York: E.P. Dutton, 1958), 113.

6. Ibid.

7. Dietrich Bonhoeffer, *The Cost of Discipleship* (New York: Touchstone, 1959), 87.

8. C. S. Lewis, *Mere Christianity* (New York: The MacMillan Company, 1960), 167.

MORE GREAT TITLES FROM MAX ANDERS

Explore these books that offer guidance on what you need to know about these vital topics for your Christian walk. Each book highlights 12 lessons that can change your life!

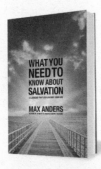
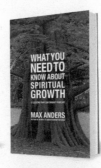
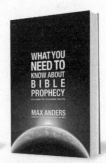
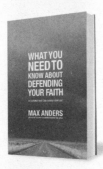

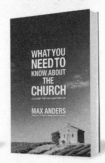
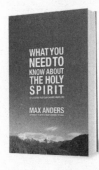

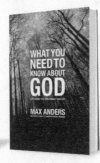
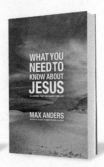

Learn more at ThomasNelson.com.

THOMAS NELSON
Since 1798